The Happy Home Circle.

Making Home Happy

By MRS. L. D. AVERY-STUTTLE

Author of "Satan's First Lie, or Man in Death;" "Poems of the Christ Life;" "The Pilgrim's Progress, a Paraphrase in Verse," etc.

REVIEW AND HERALD PUBLISHING ASSN.

WASHINGTON, D. C.

Printed in the U. S. A.

Republished by:
A B Publishing

Republished by:

AB Publishing, Inc.
Ithaca, MI 48847
www.abpub.com
Cover Artist:
James Converse

PREFACE.

THE title of this book is "Making Home Happy." It might be, "Making Home, Home;" for home is no home, unless it is happy. The home lies at the basis of all society. A land of well-regulated and happy homes, is a happy land, a land of prosperity and good government. Everything, therefore, that pertains to the preservation and improvement of the home is of vital importance. To maintain the right characteristics of domestic life, to inculcate those true principles which should govern the relations of the members of a household to each other, is necessary to the integrity of the home. And it has been thought that these lessons could be best set forth by picturing before the reader in consecutive narrative, the relations that should exist, and the lines of influence that should be guarded and cultivated, to conserve the highest ideal of the family and the home: giving it the form of an experience which would come within the limits of the attainable, and which all should seek to maintain.

It is not only on account of the larger sphere of influence herein spoken of that a right condition should be maintained in the home, but also for the good and happiness of the individual members, which should be most sedulously fostered. We trust the reader will find much in the story, told in a direct and effective manner, to interest and make the right impression on the mind, and many conditions and situations which can be studied with pleasure and profit.

PUBLISHERS

CONTENTS.

LIST OF ILLUSTRATIONS.

CHAPTER I.

A COMFORTLESS HOME.

SUPPRESSED sobs came from the haymow in the old barn, the secluded nook where Jimmie and Jennie, the eight-year-old twins, always went when anything troubled them. There they discussed their trials, and devised ways and means to avoid further difficulties. You may be sure the old mow was the scene of many earnest discussions; for, alas! the twins seemed to be always in trouble. But never did the old hiding-place harbor them when in greater distress than now. Hence the sobbing.

"See here, Jennie," sobbed Jimmie, intent on gaining his sister's sympathy; "I just *had* to tell the fib, 'cause father 'd have whipped me awful if he 'd found out I *did* set the trap that caught poor Tabby; but you see mother's cuter'n him, an' she whipped me, anyway, 'cause she said she knew I was telling a wrong story, and now she says I can't have the new kite she promised me."

By this time Jennie was crying, too, though at first there was a hard, rebellious look in the big, brown eyes. "Yes, Jimmie, I dunno how you could have done better. I don't s'pose it 's the best thing to do to tell lies; but I did n't fare any better 'n you, for mother gave me a slap, just 'cause I took your part, and *I* did n't tell any lie."

"I 'll tell you what let 's do," said Jimmie, whose sobs suddenly ceased; "let 's tell Emma; she 's older 'n us, and she has it pretty hard too."

If poor Emma could just then have heard this sympathetic remark, she would doubtless have heartily assented to its truthfulness. She was at that moment vainly trying to persuade her mother that it would be "just the thing" to allow Paul and herself a little holiday. Paul was sixteen, and old enough, he gallantly declared, to take care of himself and his sister, too. The outing was to be delightful, and the Sabbath-school class to which they belonged were all going.

"No use, Emma, you might just as well say no more. You are not going, and that 's the end of it. Seems to me it 's something all the time. It 's tease, tease, from morning till night. Pity you would n't take a little more interest in your work at home. It 'd be much better to stay at home, and study your lesson for next Sabbath," said the mother, gloomily.

The conference between Paul and his father, "the deacon," as he was familiarly known, had been still more unsatisfactory, and resulted only in many unpleasant words.

"I should think, Paul, you 'd have more sense than to leave all this work, to go to a picnic. It does seem to me that my children are very worldly," groaned the deacon.

"Worldly!" echoed Paul, contemptuously, mentally comparing his own style of worldliness with that of his father, to the great discredit of the latter. "I never have a good time like the other fellows, and I just work and work, and no matter how hard I try to please him, he never acts pleased, or lets me have a day off." Thus the lad mused sullenly, but said no more. Soon his sullen mood changed, and tossing his head in a reckless way, he trudged away whistling the air, "Give the Boy a Chance." As he walked and whistled, a new resolution came to the lad, and he determined soon to break entirely away from parental authority, which seemed to him only a galling yoke of bondage, — not a service of love.

Sim Blake was soon to leave for Chicago, intending to go from there to the far West, and had more than once suggested that Paul accompany him. Paul and Sim were becoming fast friends of late, as Deacon Beardsley and his wife had discovered, much to their regret, for Sim was one of the wildest boys in the village.

That evening after the chores were done, and the supper dishes had been washed, Emma hurried upstairs to her little room. Cheerless indeed it was with its walls bare save for the solitary picture of the bears tearing the children who had mocked Elisha. In front of the bed was a large, faded rug, which had done duty ever since she could remember; but even this room, comfortless as it appeared, was far pleasanter than Paul's, which certainly looked like anything rather than the sleeping room of the son of the most prosperous farmer in Jonesville.

Emma thought her disappointment all over in bitterness of spirit as she sat alone by the tiny window, watching the last golden fleck disappear from the sky; and when the first twinkling star came out, she lighted her little lamp, with the broken chimney and the smoky shade, and sat down to read. What? her Bible?—Alas, no: she possessed only a torn copy, which had belonged to her mother when she was a girl, and when conscience occasionally compelled her to read a chapter, she always selected a short one, excusing herself by protesting that the print was so fine. But she did not seem to realize that the print of the yellow-covered novel in her lap was still finer. The heroine in the novel was an exquisite dancer, and poor Emma longed to be distinguished in a like manner, and spent a long time in trying to devise some way to learn the art; but the more she thought of it, the more impossible it seemed, and her wretchedness increased accordingly.

After confiding their cares and sorrows to the sympathetic ear of their sister, the twins, too, had gone to bed, not to sleep the sweet sleep of childhood, but the troubled slumber that follows days filled only with harshness and unloving severity.

Deacon Beardsley and his wife would have been horrified had any one ventured to lay the blame for this state of things at their door. Of course Paul was wild, Emma was stubborn, and the twins were unmanageable; but the parents usually succeeded in getting them all to church on the Sabbath, and though their Sabbath-school lessons were almost never learned, the children were usually in their places.

Then, they always had family prayer,— unless they were in an unusual hurry in the morning, or were very tired in the evening, or had company, or something of the kind. Indeed, Deacon Beardsley thought himself a very pious and good man, and much he wondered at the waywardness of his children. Everybody admitted that he was one of the pillars of the church. It was he who proposed that a new meeting-house be built, and who became the most liberal contributor. It was he who headed the subscription-list for the famine-stricken natives of a far-distant land, and who gave a liberal sum toward building a home of refuge for the friendless, in a neighboring State. But somehow, if a poor wanderer needed a word of advice and encouragement, Brother Beardsley was the very last man whom he would seek.

Mrs. Beardsley was an echo of her husband; in fact, he seemed to have an almost unbounded influence over her. She loved her children, but she had so long kept up a cold, icy reserve toward them, that it was not to be wondered at that they sometimes questioned if she *did really* love them.

"Why do n't you ever praise us when we do well, mother?" Emma asked, one day, "as Mrs. Billings does her Mollie. I was over there the other day, and saw some nice loaves of bread, just from the oven, and Mrs. Billings said to me, 'Just see this lovely bread, Emma! Our Mollie made it, and she 's only fourteen last month;' but I don't believe it was a bit better than I do every week. I feel quite discouraged sometimes."

"My children must not expect praise from me. I consider all such things foolish and wicked. Their own good conduct must be their praise," said Mrs. Beardsley, coldly.

Poor Emma turned away with a sigh. She dared not speak the bitter words which were upon her lips.

It was the day after the Sabbath-school picnic.

2

Dark clouds had hung in the sky for a long time, and now the rain came down in torrents, making it im-

"A fellow can't have any peace of his life around here."

possible to work outdoors; so Paul was up in his cheerless room, trying to fix a revolver which his father had forbidden him to touch. A knock at his door startled him. "Is it you, Emma? how you scared me! I thought it was father. A fellow can't have any peace of his life around here; I tell you, Em, I 'm getting tired of it."

"Why don't you tell mother how you feel, Paul? maybe she could influence father to be a little easier with you. You do look just tired out and half sick."

"Tell mother? I guess not! Great comfort there 'd be in that! Father 's got her made over to suit himself exactly, and I half believe she 's as 'fraid of him as we are. I never heard him give her a loving word in my life. Maybe I 'm a queer fellow, but it does n't seem the right kind of Christianity to me."

Emma thought of the many rebuffs she had received from her mother of late, and remarking, "You 're right, Paul," she longed to throw her arms around his neck and give him a sisterly kiss; but she was afraid he would think so unheard-of a thing silly, so she only said, "Never mind, Paul; you know I am sorry, and even if — why Paul! what 's this? You don't smoke, do you? Dear me! you look sick; I 'm afraid these horrid cigarettes will kill you. What if mother knew it!"

"Hark, Em, for pity's sake! I only just got them

to-day of Sim Blake, and I took only three or four puffs when I came up here, but I declare it makes me feel mean, sure as you live."

If Emma did have a weakness toward yellow-covered novels, she certainly disliked and feared cigarettes; for she had read that they were dangerous and poisonous, and that many a boy had been ruined, body and soul, by them, and she made Paul promise that he would never touch them again.

"I 'll promise, to please you, Em. I believe you 're the only friend I 've got on earth, you and Sim Blake. By the way, I 'll tell you a secret if you 'll keep shady. Sim and I have made up to go out West, this fall, for sure. There 's no use asking father; all he cares about me is the work I can do, and I 'm *so* tired of it all. Sometimes I think if I could have a little company, like the other fellows, it would n't be so bad, but mother objects to Sim, and no one else offers to come."

"No," echoed Emma, gloomily, "and you have no place to invite them to, anyway, any more than I have,— your room is n't even as good as mine. I 'm just discouraged, myself. If father was real poor now, I would n't feel half so bad about it. I asked mother the other day if she did n't think I could have a new carpet for my room, and a fresh rug, or something, for yours; but I 'll never ask her for anything again as long as I live. She said it was sinful and extravagant, and she sighed and looked so doleful that I expect I said something saucy; anyhow, she boxed my ears soundly for *something,*— I did n't know what at the time, and I don't yet."

"Well, sis, never mind. I 'll go out West and get rich, and then I 'll take care of you and the twins; I can't help feeling sorry for Jimmie and Jennie; they get more scoldings than we do,— it 's just nag, nag, all the time."

"But someway, Paul, I hate to hear you talk about going away. Of course, I 'd like to have you get lots of money; but I don't believe money makes folks happy, after all. Look at father! he 's got money laid away, and mother has n't had a new gown in — well, since I can remember; that is, a good one. But, dear me, Paul, I 'm afraid, somehow, that it would n't be the thing to go West with Sim Blake, besides it will cost a good deal, and how would you get the money? you know father never allows you any."

"O, never fear, sis, Sim has a scheme that will bring in the stamps. I can't tell you any more."

Had Emma understood that the "scheme" was no more nor less than card-playing, for money, and that her brother had already taken his first lessons in the vice, she would have had more misgivings than ever.

Long after Emma had sought her pillow that night, did Paul's words ring in her ears,—"Sim and I are going out West." She had a real love for her brother, and now she had a vague idea that if anything should happen to him while he was gone, she would be to blame. So she set her young brain to solving the problem of how to prevent it, without letting either him or her parents know it. Should she see Sim, and try to influence him to give up the idea? She knew he would never listen to her. *O, how she longed to tell her mother!* but alas, she had never been encouraged in all her young life to make a confidant of her. What could she do? At last a happy thought occurred to her. She would tell Minnie Blair; she was the minister's daughter, and her father and mother were always so nice and kind that Emma had a vague idea that maybe if Minnie would explain it to them, *they* would know what to do.

So it came about that the next day, at school, Emma unburdened herself to her friend.

"Too bad, too bad!" sighed Elder Blair when his little daughter had made him understand the state of affairs. That evening he had a long talk with his good wife.

"I have worried for some time about that boy, Paul Beardsley," he said; "there is no bond of union or sympathy between his parents and himself. I think they intend to do right by their family, but I am satisfied that they are succeeding poorly."

"I 'm sure you are right," said the motherly little woman. "My heart aches for those children, though, as you say, Brother and Sister Beardsley are well-meaning people. There are none who give more liberally to foreign missions and to all good enterprises than they, and yet sometimes I can't help thinking of Christ's words about 'whited sepulchers.'"

"That gives me an idea," replied the minister. "Let us both ask God to help in this matter, lest we make a mistake. It is a very delicate thing to suggest to another how he should bring up his children. Perhaps I could weave something into a sermon, sometime, that would be better than a personal talk; for I have an idea that there are others who need something along this line."

And then there ascended to the Father an earnest petition, from two humble hearts, for divine wisdom and help in this matter.

CHAPTER II.

DANGER AHEAD.

ABOUT this time there was a new arrival in Jonesville. A family from the South had taken lodgings in one of the pleasantest cottages in the village, which was about half a mile from the Beardsley farm.

Captain Somerville was a very genial man, cordial and affable, but it did not take long to find that he was an infidel of the most pronounced type.

Mrs. Somerville was an invalid, who rarely left her room; so the children, Ethyl and Jack, had been left to the care of the father, principally, from early childhood; and the sad results of his training could be easily seen, especially in Jack, who lost no opportunity of declaring his belief that the Bible was worse than a fable.

It was not long before quite a friendship had sprung up between Paul and Emma Beardsley and Jack and Ethyl Somerville; and alas! the influence which the latter exerted over the former was such as to cause Deacon Beardsley and his wife many misgivings. If the influence of Sim Blake was to be dreaded, that of Jack Somerville was much worse.

But instead of quietly reasoning with Paul, and trying to influence him in the right direction by kindness and affection, Brother and Sister Beardsley took their old-time course, drew the reins tighter than ever before, and forbade their son to invite his new friend to their home or to associate with him in any way whatever. But the seeds of evil were already sown, and the harvest was sure.

It was not long before Paul contrived a way to escape from his room after the family were in bed, that in this way he might spend an evening occasionally with his new friend and Sim Blake, in the loft of a deserted building in the outskirts of the village. Here Paul took many a lesson in card-playing and cigarette-smoking; for he soon forgot the promise made to his sister. By saying "forgot," I do not mean that it had passed from his mind altogether; for conscience was not entirely dead, and in his quiet moments, it very often reproved him.

Emma and Ethyl were constantly together when

at school; and poor Minnie Blair soon discovered that she was no longer the congenial companion to Emma that she had once been, and many a tear she shed in secret over the sad change in her friend. But, unlike Emma, Minnie Blair had a never-failing counselor in her mother, to whom she at once went with this new trouble.

"O mama!" she cried, one night, rushing into her mother's room with tearful eyes, "I could n't help it. I did n't mean to hear, really I did n't, but I was in the closet after my hat, and I could n't help hearing Emma and Ethyl. They were planning how Emma could manage to go to a dance to-night at Boardman Hall, so her folks would n't know it. They finally made up that — O mama, just think of it! — Jack was to meet Emma at the Red Grocery at half-past nine, and they would go together. Emma did n't seem quite willing; but Ethyl coaxed her, and it seems that Jack has been urging her to go all the week. Ethyl is going with Paul, and, O dear!" moaned Minnie, "Emma has n't hardly spoken to me all day; she 's only a year older than I, and it seems as if fifteen is rather young to be going with young men, especially to such places."

Minnie was quite breathless by this time, and the kindly face of Mrs. Blair was a study. Surprise and sorrow were plainly written upon it.

"My child, this is a great grief to me. I have feared for Paul, but now I see that poor Emma is in even greater danger than he. But I do not see what we can do to prevent this affair to-night, without making matters worse. I have a bad headache, my dear, and can scarcely think clearly upon any subject at present; but I will talk with your father as soon as possible, and see if something can not be done to help these dear children."

Emma's miserable plan of outwitting her parents succeeded, and her love for dancing grew stronger and stronger with each indulgence; for this was only one of several escapades of the same nature within a few weeks. Each time she yielded to temptation, the voice of conscience sounded less and less distinct, until finally she began to argue that her course was right; that since no privileges were allowed her, it was only just that she should have amusement of some kind.

One day Jimmie came running into an old shed which served as a playhouse for the twins, in the greatest excitement.

"Why, Jimmie!" said Jennie; "what 's the matter now? Can't we have this place for a playhouse any more?"

"No, nothin' like it. It 's Jack Somerville!" exclaimed Jimmie, with a wise wink, calculated to impress his listener with the importance of his secret. "He 's writ a letter to Em, and he give me a lot of candy if I 'd hand it to her. Here 's some for you."

"Why, Jimmie Beardsley! I 'most know mother would n't like it," protested Jennie, as she eagerly helped herself to the bright-colored candy.

"No; she don't like nothin', 'course not; I like Jack 'cause he tells awful nice stories, and gives us candy."

"Yes; so do I, Jimmie," assented Jennie, "but mother don't, nor father, neither; maybe you 'd better be pretty sly 'bout that letter." So the wretched lesson in slyness and deception was easily learned.

Jimmie soon found a chance to slip the note into Emma's hand, which fairly trembled with excitement as she snatched it quickly from the chubby fingers, and hurried to her lonely room, where, with burning cheeks, she read it over and over again.

Children are quick to notice and read the expression of the face, and Jimmie was quite an adept at this. He had learned by watching his mother's face, about how far he could carry on his mischief without the usual whipping. In this instance he noticed the agitation of his sister, and was quite puzzled over it. The next morning, on their way to school, he and Jennie talked the matter over.

"Say, Jennie, you remember that letter Jack wrote to Em?" queried Jimmie.

"Well, I guess I do, Jimmie Beardsley," declared Jennie, as thoughts of Jack's candy quickened her memory. "Have you gone and et up all them pep'-mints?"

"'Course; but maybe Jack 'll give me a whole lot to-day. I 'll carry some more letters if he will. But my! Jennie, you just ought to 've seen Em's face; 't was redder 'n ——"

"Why, Jimmie Beardsley! maybe you 'd ought to be more quiet about it," whispered Jennie, with a sage idea that there might be some secret connected with the matter.

Minnie Blair was on her way to school also, and in passing the children, overheard just enough to convince her that Jack Somerville was keeping up some kind of secret correspondence with her friend. She loved Emma dearly, in spite of the neglect with which her old-time friend had treated her of late, and she could scarcely study all day; she was so absent-minded in her class that Miss Brown, her teacher, raised her kindly eyes in astonishment at her usually attentive pupil.

It seemed to Minnie that four o'clock would never come; but like all long days, this one finally had its end, and she found herself at last with her head on her mother's knee, sobbing out her troubles.

"I did n't mean to hear, this time, mama, any more than the other, and I *did n't* hear very much; but seems as if it 's almost providential, for I 'm sure you can do something this time to help. Of course I would n't have Emma find out that I know, for anything. It would n't do, would it, mama? But I'm real sure that bad boy is writing to Emma for no good purpose."

"I can hardly think his object *can* be a good one," replied Mrs. Blair, "as long as he is so crafty and sly about it. How sad I am that she finds no sympathy and loving companionship in her mother! Yet I am sure Sister Beardsley loves her child dearly. O why does she allow her to grow away from her arms and heart? How *can* Christian parents refuse sympathy and love to their children? I should be very jealous if I thought my little daughter preferred the society of any other person on earth to that of her mother."

"Never fear that, mama," Minnie replied, kissing her tenderly. "But I have been thinking that if you would have a good talk with Emma, you might influence her a great deal; you know she always appeared to think so much of you and papa; and, O mama! an idea strikes me this very minute, that I just believe will help us right out of our trouble.

"You remember how Emma felt when Paul told her he was going out West, and how quickly she came to us for help, don't you, mother?"

"Certainly I do, my dear," replied Mrs. Blair, with an appreciative smile; "I see your idea,—you think it would be a good plan to use Emma's love for her brother as a lever to help to lift her own feet from the mire."

"Exactly, mother mine; I think if she can be made to understand that Jack has just as bad an influence over Paul as Sim has, she 'll see her *own* danger. Don't you think so?"

"Yes, I do; and I am glad my dear daughter is trying to heed the admonition of the Saviour, to be 'wise as a serpent;' and may the dear Lord keep her always as 'harmless as a dove,'" added Mrs. Blair, tenderly.

"I will ask Emma to call to-morrow night and get the new magazine she wants to see, and then you can talk with her, mama."

So it came about that at half-past four the next afternoon, the two girls entered Mrs. Blair's pleasant sitting-room. There were rose-colored curtains at the windows, and pretty pictures, flowers, and books, and best of all, they were met by Mrs. Blair at the door, with a loving kiss for each. With gentle tact, she made Emma feel perfectly at ease. Emma could not help contrasting these pleasant surroundings with the uninviting home and the impatient greeting which always awaited her when she returned from school at night. "I don't believe I should ever care to go to another dance if my home and my mother were like Minnie Blair's," she thought.

"Now, Emma," said Mrs. Blair, in her sweet, kindly voice, "I'm not going to scold you for not coming over oftener of late, but I have missed you."

Just then Elder Blair called Minnie into the library, leaving Mrs. Blair and Emma alone. An earnest prayer from a burdened heart sped swiftly upward for help "just now."

"By the way, Emma," Mrs. Blair remarked, as she handed the girl the magazine she wanted, "has Paul said any more to you about going out West? Perhaps you may think we have forgotten our promise to do all we can to help you to save your brother, but I assure you we do not forget him in our prayers, for we can see the danger he is in."

"He has n't said anything about it lately," said Emma, uneasily, "though really, Mrs. Blair, I think he intends to go."

"I have been wondering if it might not be possible that young Somerville has an influence over him that is perhaps as harmful as that of Sim Blake."

"O Mrs. Blair! how could that be possible?" exclaimed Emma, blushing. "Paul and Jack are great friends, I know; but Jack appears such a gentleman. It does n't seem hardly as if — and yet ——"

"And yet he, as well as his father, is an unbeliever — an infidel. I very much wish we could in some way lead both Jack and Paul, yes, and poor Sim Blake as well, into the fold of the Good Shepherd."

"Well, I 'll tell you, Mrs. Blair," said Emma, dubiously, "the fact is, I can't blame Paul so very much; he is completely discouraged. I think he 'd be a real good boy if he had a nice, pleasant home, and if mother and father 'd sympathize with him. I don't know as I ought to say it; but I know Paul's just lonesome — so am I, for that matter."

By the time Emma had finished her pathetic little speech, there were tears in Mrs. Blair's eyes. "I feel very sorry for you, my child, but I am sure there is a way out of this trouble," she said. "Your parents certainly love you; of this you need have no doubt, although they may not manifest it in the way in which you would have them. Have you ever tried the power and comfort of prayer, my dear? Did you ever think how the pitying Christ loves you?"

"I don't know, Mrs. Blair. How am I to be sure that Christ loves me? I read a text the other day that says, 'Like as a father pitieth his children, so the Lord pitieth them that fear him,' and I thought when I read it, that if the Lord did n't pity us any more than our father does, he would n't pity us very much."

"Well," said Mrs. Blair, putting her arm around Emma, "try to forget all the hard, bitter things, and remember what they have done for you. They are surely right in not wanting their children to associate with young people who may prove their ruin, both in this world and in the next. Young girls are especially in danger of being led astray, and should certainly avoid too great intimacy with young men, even with those whom they may consider above reproach, and certainly with those whose lives show us that they have no connection with the Master. It is quite as impossible for one to handle coals nowadays, and not be burned, as it was in the days of the inspired writer. I hope my dear young friend will not be offended at what I say; for it all comes from a heart filled with the tenderest love for her."

"O Mrs. Blair!" and the fair face was buried on

the motherly shoulder, "if only mother 'd talk to me so, I could stand anything — just anything! I 've felt almost desperate lately, and thought it did n't much matter what became of me. I know I've been foolish," and her cheeks burned as she thought, "What if Mrs. Blair knew of Jack's letters! I ought not to have anything in my heart that I would be ashamed to have known." "Yes, I've been foolish," she continued, "but I *am* worried about Paul. I hope you 'll pray for him; I believe in *your* prayers."

"O Mrs. Blair!" and the fair face was buried on the motherly shoulder.

Before Emma laid her head on her pillow that night, she was sure of two things: first, that she had a friend in Mrs. Blair; and second, that it would be better to be a little less intimate with the Somervilles.

That evening Mrs. Blair whispered a few earnest words to her husband, to which he replied: —

"Yes, I think the time has come for me to preach the sermon I 've had in my heart so long. I will give it next Sabbath; and may God grant his Spirit," he added earnestly.

CHAPTER III.

A MESSAGE FROM HEAVEN.

THE next Sabbath, Deacon Beardsley and all the family were in their seats. The minister arose, and with unwonted earnestness and fervor, read the parable of the prodigal son. It seemed that there was, indeed, an unseen Presence filling the little meeting-house, and subduing all hearts by its divine influence, as the wonderful love of the All-father was portrayed.

"'When he was yet a great way off, his father saw him, and had compassion, and ran, and fell on his neck, and kissed him.'

"'When he was yet *a great way off!'* The pitying Father does not wait for his sons and daughters to get *near* to him," said the persuasive voice in the pulpit, "but he sees them when yet a great way off. Sin makes a wide gulf between the Father and our souls, but O, how quick he is to recognize the first faint desire on our part to return to him! He sees us when we are a long way from him, and, seeing us, his great heart of love throbs with compassion and pity for us, and *he runs to meet us.* The infinite love of our Heavenly Father could not be portrayed in better language.

"But how does this compare with the manner in which we who are parents treat our own beloved children who have wandered, and perhaps justly merited our disapprobation?"

Deacon Beardsley's head bowed low, and his heart beat hard under the searching question. Could it be possible that he had been a trifle too severe with Paul? The hard lines on the sunburned face began to soften.

"It is natural for the human heart to seek to appear well before the world," continued the minister. "It is not that any of us gives too much for the conversion of the heathen, but are we faithful in our families? Do we teach, by our example, the gospel of love? Are we bringing our sons and our daughters as a sweet offering to lay at the Master's feet? or are we, by our hard, unsympathetic nature, driving them farther and farther from us — and so from the church of Christ?

"The father in the parable was very affectionate. It was not enough that the son had returned home. No reproaches awaited him — nothing but love and tenderness. O, are there none of my dear hearers to-day who need to make the journey to meet some loved one — some wayward prodigal? I entreat you, in God's name, make haste! *run!* Eternal consequences hang in the balance.

"The father in the parable did not appear to think it unseemly to *kiss* his son,— and that son not a child, but a young man, who had squandered the father's hard-earned money. How many would have met the unhappy wanderer with, 'I told you so! I knew you 'd be glad enough to come back!' O, the value of a loving, tender, appreciative kiss from the parent to the child! We have failed to enter into the feelings of our children; we have forgotten our own childhood, and our own longings after love and sympathy."

Paul glanced sidewise at Emma, and Emma winked hard to keep back the tears; for she could remember that when she was real little, mother and father did n't seem to be so busy, and then sometimes Paul and she were put to bed with a good-night kiss and a pretty story; but that seemed so long ago!

The twins appeared to comprehend that the minister was talking about its being everybody's duty to love one another better, and so Jimmie bent over, and slyly imprinted a hearty kiss on his little sister's rosy cheek. Of course every one smiled, and the minister said he hoped the older people would all be as ready to profit by the sermon as were the children.

"I tell you the truth, my brethren," continued he, "there are too many whited sepulchers in the church of Christ to-day. Shall there not be among us a deep searching of heart to see if, in the sight of God, this is the case with us? Shall we turn about? Shall our hearts be so full of that peace which passeth understanding that instead of a frown, a smile shall transfigure our faces, and our children shall see, by our kind words and affectionate manner, that we love them?

"What!" continued he, "shall we reserve the sweet smile and the kindly word for a stranger, and give to our own only stern looks and gruff words? Is that the way the Master did?

"In the parable the father is so loving and kind that he not only runs to meet his son, and kisses him most affectionately, but he also commands the servants to bring the best robe and put it on him, and to put shoes upon his feet."

In spite of herself, Sister Beardsley thought of the new carpet Emma wanted so much for her bedroom, and the deacon blushed as he thought of the cheap suit of clothes he had refused to buy for Paul that very week.

Emma looked over to her brother, where he sat in his threadbare garments, and then at her father.

"Well," she thought, "Paul's clothes are no poorer than father's, and mother's gown is just as shabby as mine, and so I don't suppose I ought to complain," and her heart grew tender under the influence of the Holy Spirit.

"What does this teach?" continued the pastor. "Does it teach a lesson of extravagance? — Far from it. Shall we dress our children and ourselves in the height of fashion? The parable teaches nothing of the kind.

"What does it teach? Has this wonderful lesson of the Master's fallen upon heedless ears and unfeeling hearts? Surely it would teach, first of all, that love, pure and sweet, should enter into the home life of his children. Home is no place for angry words. Satan would be glad to make every home a hell, but God wants each one to be a miniature heaven. Fathers, while you have been providing for the bodily comfort of your sons and daughters, you have neglected the sweeter work of feeding their hearts with affection and love; and, in truth, they are *starving for it.* Mothers, in the name of the Master, I entreat you, rescue the prodigal. You can reach him. The arms of love will reach a long way and span a wide gulf. Away with this icy reserve! Away with the religion which has in it so little of the love of the Master!

"We have heard that when once a boat is caught in the rapids above Niagara Falls, human help is vain. The time to help, the time to pull on the oars of faith and love mightily, is when the boat begins first to drift. Brethren and sisters, our boys and our girls are drifting. I can see them nearing the rapids. Shall they go over to eternal ruin?"

"God forbid!" groaned the deacon.

"What shall we do then? I feel persuaded that there is a lesson which the Master would teach us, that we have not thought of. Perhaps he would have us make our homes so attractive and so filled with the sunshine of love, that our daughters would consider home the brightest spot on earth, and that our sons would prefer the cheerful sitting-room to the billiard-hall, and the society of mother and sisters to that of the down-town rowdy. I said 'perhaps.' My brethren, I am *sure* the Great Teacher has a lesson for us along these lines. Much I fear that our sons and daughters are going to destruction before our very eyes, and we know it not.

"Did you ever notice how brilliantly lighted the billiard-hall and saloon are kept by the cunning owner? Why does n't he keep his rooms dark and cheerless? He knows they would not attract customers thither if he did. The devil uses every means to allure the unwary into his net. Music, with its seductive power; pictures, with their atmosphere of cheer; books, with the witching fascination which the most gifted writers have woven into their thrilling tales,— nothing is considered too sacred and beautiful to use as an allurement whereby the young are led on and on away from the faith of integrity into the highway of ruin. Even sweet poetry is turned from its rightful use, which, as one has truthfully expressed it, should be only —

"'To make the souls of mortals pure and white,
And fair and sinless as the angels be,
To keep the fire on love's altar bright,—
This be thy mission, O sweet poetry'—

turned, I say, from its holy mission, and made to do the devil's errands.

"And shall we be less careful to use our best endeavors to draw our loved ones to Christ, by using every means in our power to this end? When shall our homes cease to be mere boarding-houses? When shall our youth find in father and mother the true companionship for which their young hearts yearn? When *shall* we learn that though we give our body to be burned and have not charity — love, sweet love — it profiteth us nothing?"

Many "amens" were heard from the attentive worshipers, and there was a bright tear in Sister Beardsley's eye and a slight tremble of her hand as she turned the leaves of her hymn-book in an absent-minded manner. The twins noticed the tear, and looked at each other wonderingly. Deacon Beardsley did not notice it; for the solemn words kept ringing in his ears: "Our sons and our daughters are going to destruction, and we know it not."

"Draw them to Christ," said the pastor, "by the cords of love and sympathy. Teach Mary and John that there is no other earthly ear so willing to listen to all their plans and to all their troubles,— no matter how small, they are not small to them,— and no other earthly heart so full of love and sympathy as are father's and mother's. Make home attractive; let us learn how to do this without being extravagant. Shall we be wise as serpents? Shall we learn to catch our sons and our daughters with guile?[1] Let us bring hither the best robe for our wandering loved ones; let us show them love and affection; let us win their confidence by showing them the tenderness due them. Perhaps we can save them yet; perhaps our lips may yet sing joyfully the happy refrain: 'This my son was dead, and is alive again; he was lost, and is found.'"

One, two, three. What was that? — tears? can it be possible? The head of Deacon Beardsley was bowed low, and something between a groan and a sob was distinctly audible. The sermon closed with the beautiful song: —

"There were ninety and nine that safely lay
In the shelter of the fold;
But one was out on the hills away,
Far, far from the gates of gold."

Then there was given opportunity for testimonies.

[1] 2 Cor. 12: 16

CHAPTER IV.

A GREAT TRANSFORMATION.

THERE was an expectant hush in the little meeting-house. The summer sunshine streamed in through the tiny window back of the pulpit, and painted a halo of golden light about the bowed head of the parson, as Deacon Beardsley arose to his feet.

"My brethren, I feel sure that the Holy Spirit prompted this sermon which we have heard. It is the blessed gospel of love. I am sure God has been speaking to me, and I am fully determined to listen to his voice. I feel like making the prayer of the poor publican, 'God be merciful to me a sinner,' my own.

"I have a confession to make, and a most humble one; but it is not one to be made in public, although toward mankind, in general, I have not manifested the love of the Master. I have lacked the charity that 'suffereth long and is kind.' I have forgotten 'to be pitiful,' to 'be courteous.' My confession will be made to my own family. Brethren, I am alarmed! When

"My Brethren, I Have a Confession to Make!"

the King shall come, and call me to render an account of my stewardship, what if I be not able to say to him," and the deacon's voice grew tremulous, "Here am I and the children whom thou hast given me?"

After their return home that Sabbath day, Deacon Beardsley sought a quiet place in the barn, and there, in the sweet-scented hay, he poured out his soul to God as he had not done for years before. When at last he arose and sought his family, the hard lines had all gone out of his face, and the peace of God rested there. He had the sweet assurance of forgiveness. As he opened the sitting-room door, his wife stepped from the closet. Her eyes were red with weeping, and there was an unusual tremble in her voice as she said, questioningly, "Well, father?"

"Well, my wife, do you think it is too late to begin all over again — to begin anew?" and he drew her closer, and kissed her faded cheek tenderly.

Paul was just putting on his hat to take a stroll, hoping to meet Sim or Jack somewhere, and Emma was trying to do up her hair in the latest style before a broken looking-glass.

"Wait a little, my son; don't go out yet. Where are Jennie and Jimmie? O, here they are! Sit down, mother. There, little ones," said the deacon as he drew up a rocking-chair, "I guess you are not too big for father to hold;" and Jennie climbed awkwardly to an unaccustomed perch on her father's chair-arm, while Jimmie sat on his knee, wondering what was going to happen next.

"My children," the deacon began, "my *dear* children, it breaks my heart when I tell you that I am certain there have been many times in the past few years when you have doubted my love for you, and I fear with good reason. But I *do* love you. God forgive me for not better proving it to you. Paul, my boy, I have been hard and unsympathetic toward you. I had almost forgotten that I was a boy like you, once,— not so very long ago, either, *was* it, mother? I have not shown the tender love for my daughter that I have really felt. It is not my nature; but I believe God will give me a new nature in the place of this evil one,— for evil it certainly is. I have been hasty and unkind, and have not allowed you to enjoy innocent amusements, which I now see it was perfectly right you should have had. O my children! 'Whereas I was blind, now I see.'"

"God forgive me *too!*" moaned Mrs. Beardsley,

"I have been no help to you or to my children. I have refused them everything and granted them nothing. I might have made home more pleasant for them. O my dear children! if it is not too late, let mother have a little corner in your hearts yet. That sermon has opened my eyes as they were never opened before. O, if it could only have come sooner! Do you think it is too late, Paul?" she cried, piteously. "Do you think you can confide in mother just a little, and forgive her for the past?" Her arms were around him, and her kisses fell fast on his cheek.

"Never you mind, mother; your 're all right; I suppose I 've been mean and aggravating, but I did n't think any one cared for me; I ought to have known better, of course," and he snatched his cap and started toward the barn, with an expression of both astonishment and incredulity upon his face.

Emma's tears were falling fast now, as she sat on a low stool at her mother's knee. Her conscience was busy at work. She wondered that she had not noticed how thin and pale her mother looked, or how gray her father had grown of late. After all, her parents were very dear to her, and her resolutions grew stronger to do better, and to be a help to them.

"There, there Emma, child," said the deacon, "father does n't want you to cry any more; it will spoil those blue eyes that look so much as yours used to, mother; it does n't seem as if I ever noticed it before."

How strange her father's voice sounded, and how wonderful it all seemed! Was it a dream?

Jimmie and Jennie had slid down from their father's lap, and hurried off to the barn, where they could talk it all over.

"Say, Jimmie Beardsley, look here!" said Jennie. "*he* kissed me two times — Jimmie Beardsley — *two times!*"

"Yep," assented Jimmie, "*all hisself,* his own self! and he squeezed me like I could n't breathe. I guess something 's going to happen."

"I 'most know there is," replied his sister, in an awestruck whisper, "'cause mother never scolded one bit when we ran out. She just kissed us, and cried and cried."

Paul got the benefit of their conversation as he sat on a bunch of hay, with head bowed on his hand, wondering if father and mother *would* care so very much if he went out West. "I don't wonder the twins are astonished; I guess it pretty near takes their breath. *If it only lasts,*" he added.

That night, with her cheek close to her mother's, Emma told her about Paul's going West. Mrs. Beardsley was frightened, and her voice trembled as she inquired, anxiously, "Have you known about this very long, my daughter?"

"Not so very," said Emma, hesitatingly; "I wanted to tell you before, but ——"

"Yes, I understand, my child. Mother 's going to be more companionable after this, I hope."

That evening, with many tears, Mrs. Beardsley told her husband about the new trouble which threatened them. "I fear we 've about lost our hold on Paul," she moaned. "O my poor boy!"

"Cheer up, mother. I hope something can yet be done to save him," replied the deacon. "I think, for *one* thing, we must try to make home so pleasant for him that he will not care to go. That 's what Brother Blair said in the sermon.

"God helping us, we can try. O, why were we blinded so long to the best interests of our children?"

At length it was decided to give Paul a surprise. Emma was taken into the secret, of course, and many were the little schemes and plans devised to prevent Paul's "finding out." The next Thursday was his seventeenth birthday, and it was thought best to plan the surprise for that day. Mrs. Beardsley and Emma went to the village on Monday to make the needed purchases, so they would have time to make every arrangement before the great event. There was a pretty new carpet, with bright roses set in a dark ground, and Emma determined to have the windows dressed just like those in Minnie Blair's dainty room. The room was dingy,— it had not been papered since Emma could remember,— so they selected new paper of a delicate shade that would match the curtains and carpet.

As Paul was going to Edenville on business for his father that Wednesday, and could not return before noon of the next day,— his birthday,— everything was arranged to be ready to paper and settle his room during his absence. Even the twins were at last let into the secret; and although they had constantly to be watched lest, in the exuberance of their joy, they might say something which would lead to the discovery of the plot, they behaved very sensibly in the main. and were really helpful.

Of course Paul could not help noticing that there was a great difference in the home atmosphere since the last Sabbath. His father was much kinder and more considerate of his feelings, and his mother was getting really tender toward him. He noticed, also, that someway the twins were either less ingenious in devising their usual amount of mischief, or else no one seemed to have the time to scold them.

"Well, Em," he exclaimed, catching his sister by the arm, "the Somervilles are going South on a visit. Mrs. Somerville is n't as well as usual, and the Captain thinks it will help her."

"Well, that 's sudden," was Emma's only reply; but she wondered if it was not almost providential, on Paul's account as well as her own.

"Yes, they 'll be gone a number of weeks. But say, sis," said Paul, changing the subject, "it seems awful nice, does n't it? queer though; a fellow can actually take a long breath, lately, without anybody's rising to object. I wish I was *sure* this state of things would last. If I thought 't would, I'd ——"

"What, Paul? what would you do?" questioned Emma, eagerly.

"Do? why I 'd stay at home,— that 's what I 'd

do. Sim would be disappointed, of course; but — say, sis, do you suppose father 'd care, or mother?" but before Emma could reply, he added, sullenly, "O, it won't last long — it can't. I know my father's temper too well. Then mother, too,— she can't hold out long this way."

"O pshaw, Paul! I just believe, now, that father and mother really mean it. I overheard mother praying in her room to-day, and if you 'd heard what I did, I guess you 'd think it would last."

"O well, if it lasts for a month, I shall begin to believe there 's something in it. I tell you, Em Beardsley, I don't know about it. If you believe it 's genuine, I suppose you 'll have to quit sneaking off to parties on the sly; for of course you don't want to make them feel bad."

"I have quit," replied Emma, meekly.

"Well, I 'll 'quit,' too, after I 'm convinced," and with a whistle which was intended to express to his sister his utter contempt for anybody who could be so easily "convinced," he walked leisurely down the path toward the barn.

At last Wednesday morning came, and Paul was almost ready to go to Edenville.

" I guess, mother," said Emma, " we 've got everything done now that we can do till Paul gets his back turned. I wish he 'd hurry. Dear me! seems as if he 'd never get started. I 'm so glad he 's got to be gone all night."

" Yes, 't is lucky," replied Mrs. Beardsley. " That 's your father's scheme. He did intend to go himself, but he made up his mind that Paul could do the business just as well, and then it would give us a chance to fix things up."

" Father 's a darling! " exclaimed Emma.

" Do you think so, daughter? " and Emma blushed a rosy red as she caught her father's twinkling eye. " Do you really think so? That warms father's heart wonderfully, child."

" I did n't think you 'd hear my nonsense. I thought I saw you at the barn," she stammered.

" Bring me the lap-robe, will you, Emma? " called Paul. " I thought I had it. Hurry up, sis, it 's a long way to Edenville."

" That 's so, Paul," she said, handing him the robe, " but I begin to think it is n't such a very long way to *Eden*," she added.

" Say, Em, *queer, is n't it?* "

"Yes, but dear me, Paul, do drive on; you 'll not get started to-day; and *I 'm* in a hurry."

"Yes, I 've noticed you were lately. I wonder what 's up. Good-by."

"Good-by, Paul," answered Emma, and he drove away, wondering what made Emma in such a hurry to get him started. She herself ran to the house, where so much was waiting to be done, wondering if Paul did mistrust anything, and what he would say when he came home.

CHAPTER V.

A BIRTHDAY SURPRISE.

THAT day and till noon of the next were busy ones at Deacon Beardsley's. The dingy walls of Paul's room had at last been papered by careful though unaccustomed hands, and the last tack in the new carpet had been driven. A nice white spread covered the bed, and some lace tidies ornamented the bureau, which had been given a coat of varnish. There was a pretty chenille spread for the stand, upon which had been placed two or three books, including a beautiful Bible, with Paul's name written in his mother's handwriting on the fly-leaf of each. When the last picture had been hung, and the last finishing touch given to the rose-colored curtains, which were Emma's especial delight (for were they not precisely like Minnie Blair's?), Emma and her mother stood in the doorway to survey the work of their hands.

"*What* will Paul say!" Emma exclaimed for the hundredth time.

"Do you think he will be pleased, daughter?" said

Mrs. Beardsley, with a tremble in her voice. "Do you think we are too late to save him? O my poor boy! I think it will kill me if he goes away out West with that bad boy."

"Never fear, wife," cried the deacon, cheerfully, "we 'll keep him, yet. But really, I 'd no idea a few dollars and a heart full of love *could* make such a transformation."

"My! but Paul won't believe his own eyes," piped Jimmie, from one corner of the enchanted room.

"Guess he won't, Jimmie Beardsley!" replied Jennie, from her perch on the deacon's shoulder.

The twins were beginning to get really acquainted with their father, much to their delight, and Jennie explained a little later, to Jimmie, "We 're real 'quainted, father 'n me; he *in*quested me to get in his lap, his own self." Jennie had of late acquired a notion of using words which were rather too large for her, and with poor success; but when, on the present occasion, Jimmie offered a feeble criticism, she stoutly affirmed, "I 'm just as old as you be, Jimmie Beardsley."

"Really," said Mrs. Beardsley, "I did not know

Paul's room *did* look so bad, but now it rather puts yours to shame, Emma."

"Never mind, daughter, it 's your turn next," said the deacon, who felt fully repaid for his suggestion by a happy smile, and a hearty, "Thank you, father."

Paul was expected home at about one o'clock. It seemed to the twins that it was the longest morning they ever knew. Emma and her mother were far too busy to note the passage of time. The table had been ornamented with bouquets, and was loaded with the good things which had been carefully prepared.

Finally, as one o'clock drew near, the twins could endure the suspense no longer; so Jimmie mounted the fence, and climbed from there into a large apple-tree, where he could see a long distance down the road, while Jennie, not to be outdone, took her seat on the barn-yard gate-post.

At last a joyful cry from the two watchers announced that Paul was coming. The twins could be restrained no longer. Down the road flew four little feet, and —"O Paul Beardsley! *we know something!*" was echoed in concert from two little throats. Jimmie climbed up behind, while Paul helped Jennie to a seat beside him, as with a voice trembling with excitement, she said, "Hurry up, Paul! mother 's all dressed up, and we 've got a awful good dinner,— posies and everything,— and ——"

"O Paul Beardsley! We know something!"

"Now, Jennie Beardsley," interrupted Jimmie, indignant that his sister had outdone him in divulging the important news, "you had n't ought to tell all you know; mother said so."

"I have n't, Jimmie Beardsley! I have n't told a

thing about his bedroom, nor the carpet, nor the curtains, nor nothin', there now! nor I sha 'n't."

"Why, what 's the matter with the children? are they crazy?" Paul asked his father; as they drove into the yard. The deacon wisely ignored the question, and after asking Paul if he had had good luck, told him he would take care of the horses, if his son would go into the house and rest a bit before dinner, as he was sure he must be tired.

"How thoughtful father *is* getting!" mused Paul, as he opened the dining-room door and looked in. An ominous silence reigned. His eye caught sight of the table. How beautiful it looked! there must be company sure, he thought, "Mother!" he called.

In a moment there were two pairs of arms around his neck, and hearty kisses were imprinted upon his cheeks, while the air fairly rang with, "I wonder who 's seventeen to-day — seventeen to-day?"

"I suppose I am; but dear me! why mother! did you make all these fixings for me? She did n't, did she, Em? I declare the table's set fit for the President."

"Well," said the deacon, just entering from the barn, "let 's see if everything tastes as good as it looks."

The twins were almost unmanagable, but after the excitement had gone down, they seated themselves at the table; and the deacon, with trembling voice, asked the blessing of the Lord upon the food and upon each member of the little flock, mentioning them each in turn. He thanked God that they had been spared to one another so long, and prayed that his dear boy, now entering upon a new year of his life, might be led to devote every coming year to the service of the Master.

Paul was sure it would never do to let any one see the tears which sprung to his eyes, so he hastily turned his head to brush them away; and before the meal was ended, he had half decided that it would be a poor idea, maybe, after all, to run away with Sim Blake.

The twins finished their dinner unusually soon, and were in great haste for Paul to leave the table; but he seemed to be in no hurry.

"Come, Paul, hustle up!" called Jimmie.

"He 's eating hisself to death," Jennie indignantly asserted, when he had ignored the dozenth invitation to "come on."

At last all seemed satisfied. "Let 's go up-stairs now, my boy," said the deacon; and the procession started, headed by the twins, closely followed by the hero of the occasion, greatly mystified.

"There now!" cried Jennie, throwing open the door, and bounding inside. "What do you think of this *splendificent* room, Paul Beardsley?"

"Goodness, Em! Who did it? Where am I? It is n't *my room! My!* what a place for a boy to sit and spend his evenings! Really, you don't mean it; it can't be for *me?*"

"Yes, yes," echoed every one in concert. "Do you forget who 's seventeen years old to-day?"

"Come, see these pretty books and this Bible; mother writ your name in it yesterday; me and Jennie, we saw her, did n't we Jen? *My!*" added Jimmie, "I wish 't *I* was seventeen!"

"Well, mother; I don't know who I 'm to thank, — all of you, I suppose. I guess I can't bear much more," he added, with a suspicious tremble in his voice; "somehow it breaks a fellow up." "O," he thought, "I would n't have father and mother know of that wretched Western fever for the world,— nor a hundred other things, either," and his cheek burned as he thought of the number of times he had left this same little room, unknown to his parents, to meet Sim and Jack. "I feel as if I must thank you all around again; it 's all I can do," he added humbly.

"We 're so glad it pleases you, Paul," said the deacon. "The Lord willing, it 's only a beginning. I feel as if I 'd been neglecting my loved ones all my life, but whereas I was blind, now I see."

"*I* feel as if we have the loveliest father! but we have n't half appreciated him, have we, Paul?" said Emma, growing bold in her enthusiasm.

"No, we just have n't, Em, nor we have n't half appreciated mother, either. I 'm a great heedless, rough boy; not worth half the pains you 've taken; but I 'd be a brute if I did n't appreciate it, and I do.

"Come, mother," said the deacon, "come, children; Paul must be left alone to enjoy his room by himself now. I know about how he feels. I have n't felt so like a boy, myself, in years."

It was a task to persuade the twins that Paul could get along without their society for a short time; but at last he closed the door softly, and found himself alone. The first thing he did was to seat himself in the easy chair, with its bright cushion and snowy tidy. Then putting his feet on the ottoman, he leaned his head on his hand, and thought out loud: —

"Yes, Em is right; they 're converted. I believe in such conversion as this, too. I feel ashamed because I was so skeptical. I 'm ashamed of myself, anyway; I 've been an awful mean boy. I just have n't the heart to leave home now. There 's mother,— she acts as if she thought her eyes of me, and I believe she does. If this sort of thing holds out,— but of course I ought to be reasonable,— if it holds out half way, I 'll be satisfied. Here I 've been distrusting them, and they doing all this for me! O Paul Beardsley, you 're a mean fellow — you are!"

Then he rose slowly, and walking over to the window, touched the beautiful drapery almost reverently. Everything in the room was carefully inspected. The soft sunlight came through the curtains, and gave a rosy tint to the dainty bed, with its snowy cover, which Emma had taken such pains to arrange; and the whole was reflected in the shining mirror, the first he had ever had in his life.

Paul seated himself again in his easy chair, and again began his reflections: "I 'm a selfish bear to enjoy all this alone, the very best in the house. Just see father's and mother's room, and Em's, too; she deserves this more than I do. I 'll whack up; that 's what I 'll do. But then, I suppose mother 'll get some more knickknacks for the rest of the house,— hope she will,— but it is n't *that* so much as the *love* that 's back of it. Hurrah! but is n't it fine!" and he flung his handkerchief into the air, and would have danced, only every thing seemed so sacred.

"I always *did* know that religion was a good thing to have, and *they 've got it* — the genuine article. They are just as unselfish as they can be. Mother works hard, and father too. Now they 're getting old, and its *your* business, Paul Beardsley," he continued, looking at his reflection in the glass, "to be a *man.*" I suppose the thing to do would be to thank the Lord for all this,— my! but father's prayer at the table *was* beatuiful,"— and the overjoyed lad walked to the bedside, and bent one knee reverently. Then, with a blush, he rose quickly, and crossed to the other side of the room, saying slowly: "I don't suppose God cares to hear *me,* I 'm so mean and selfish. If I was as good as the rest — but I 've smoked, even after I promised Em I would n't; and it was only last week I played euchre for the cigars, with Sim and Jack. I know it would kill mother if she knew it. O, I 've been awful mean; God wouldn't hear *my* prayers."

Poor Paul! He had not yet learned that Christ came not to call the righteous, but sinners, to repentance; but the Holy Spirit had begun its blessed work, and when at last he came down-stairs, and putting his arms around his mother's neck, kissed her tenderly there was already such a light in his eyes that Jennie whispered to Jimmie, "See Paul! I wonder if he 's been praying."

CHAPTER VI.

GROWING IN GRACE.

TRUE love, the love of Christ, has a wonderfully transforming power; it transforms the lives of those who cherish it. The Beardsley household was an example of its mighty power in the hearts of the deacon and his wife. It was not that they were free from temptation,—the enemy never allows us too easy a victory,—nor that they never failed; but they were *growing in grace,* and it was not many weeks before the last lingering doubt that they were in earnest, and that, indeed, old things had passed away, and all things had become new, was removed from Paul's mind.

Little by little, each dingy room in the large house underwent such a renovating and brightening up that the twins said it was just like the fairy stories in their book.

Emma's room was not one whit behind Paul's, as her father had generously declared it must not be; and the little fine-printed Testament on the stand had long ago given place to a nicely bound copy of the sacred Word, which, I am glad to say, already gave good evidence of every-day use. As a natural consequence, novel-reading became less and less a delight to her, until it was entirely abandoned. At first she had ceased the practice because she could not bear to displease her parents, when they had done so much for her; but afterward, wholly from a sense of the evils which she knew would follow.

The Somervilles had just returned from the South; and when Jack and Ethyl heard of the change in their old-time friends, they were considerably ill at ease. Emma, too, was sure she should not feel as much at home in their society as she used to, and wondered how she ever *could* have slighted Minnie Blair.

"I 'm sure," Paul declared to his sister, "it 's twice as nice at home as it is skulking around nights, and then feeling like a sneak all the time."

"Hallo, Paul!" called Sim, one day. "What 's come over you? converted, eh? well, ain't that a good joke? I heard the deacon had got considerable stirred up, lately; pretty good thing, I guess; maybe 't will make him more sociable," he sneered, "but it does n't seem to work that way with you," he added, sullenly.

"Why, I ain't hardly seen you for a month. Lost your Western fever, I suppose."

"Well, if you 'll give a fellow a chance, I 'll try to answer some of your questions," replied Paul, blusning; for he really did n't know how to manage Sim. The fact was, this boy had once had a great influence over him, and he felt it yet. But Paul determined to be at least an honest boy, and to make a clean breast of it.

"I 'm glad I have this chance to explain, Sim. No; I 'm not converted. Wish I was, for that matter, if it would have as good an effect on me as it does on my parents."

"'*My parents!*'" sneered Sim. "You seem to be a deal fonder of them than you were."

"Yes, sir, *my parents;* and you want to be kind of careful how you mention them, Simeon Blake. I don't deserve half they 've done for me, I can tell you that; and it makes me ashamed every time I think about that running away business. *No, sir;* I 'm not going with you, and I 'd advise you to stay at home, Sim."

"Yes! pretty home I 've got to stay to, is n't it? Old man drunk all the time, mother dead years ago,

— guess it 's a good thing,— grandmother cross as sixty (say, Paul, I don't believe granny ever spoke a kind word to me in her life), hungry as a bear half the time,— *no, sir!* I 'm going, and that ends it; but when I strike it rich, you 'll be sorry you did n't come along."

"I feel as if I *had* 'struck it rich' every time I go into my room. You just ought to see it, Sim. Mother and Em have fixed it all up, you know," said Paul, who thought his room the nicest in the house.

"O, well; 't is n't noways likely your father 'd have *me* in his grand house for a minute." Sim had been highly indignant when a long time before, Deacon Beardsley had forbidden him, as well as Jack Somerville, to call on Paul at his house.

"Well, Sim, I 'm going to run the risk of inviting you, anyway I know father 'd want me to do it. Come over this very evening,— they 're nice and long now,— and trust me for a good time."

"Not much! catch me! the deacon might forget his religion, and give me a horse-whipping."

"Well, do as you like, of course; but if you come, you 'll be treated well. My father is a gentleman as well as a Christian."

"O, well; we won't argue that point. Of course I have my own opinion."

When the two boys parted, Paul had no idea that Sim would accept his invitation; but curiosity was a prominent feature in Sim's make-up, and he had about half decided, before the sun went down, that he would go over and see Paul's room.

At the supper table that evening, Paul told his experience with Sim. It seemed so good to feel free to talk, and tell all the little occurences of the day, feeling sure of warm sympathy.

"Poor Sim!" replied Mrs. Beardsley. "I feel really sorry for him. I hardly think he 'll do our Paul any harm, will he, father? Can't we afford to give the poor, motherless boy a welcome, if he should come?"

"Lord bless the poor boy! I meant him no harm. You did right to invite him, Paul." But a tear glistened in the deacon's eye as he earnestly repeated: "'One thing I know, that, whereas I was blind, now I see.'"

The family had scarcely left the table when a knock was heard at the back door. Sim Blake's curiosity had prevailed.

It happened that the deacon opened the door. There stood Sim, with his hands in his pockets and a sheepish look on his face, and stammeringly inquired for Paul.

"Come right in, Simeon!"

"Come right in, Simeon, come right in. Paul 's in the sitting-room," said the deacon as he led the way into the brightly lighted room, so different from what Sim remembered it to be.

"Is that you, Sim? glad you made up your mind to come over." Sim always managed to dress pretty well, and had good natural ability, and, thanks to the village school, a tolerably good education, which partly accounted for the fact that boys like Jack Somerville and Paul Beardsley had so intimately associated with him.

"We are glad to see you, Simeon," said Mrs. Beardsley, heartily.

"Yes, of course we are," added the deacon. "You are perfectly welcome to come at any time you like. I don't see things as I used to, my boy. By the good Lord's help I am going to try to live a little nearer like the divine Pattern. *He* never forbade people to come to see him, if I read the good book rightly."

"I wanted to see Paul's room," stammered Sim.

"All right, come right up," said Paul, as he led the way, with perhaps a trifle of pardonable exultation in his heart, while Sim followed, admiringly.

"I guess he 'll see that my father is a gentleman. That little speech of his was simply splendid. *My!* I 'd no idea my father *was* so grand," thought Paul, as he opened the door of his cherished apartment.

"Whew!" he exclaimed, "is all this *your own?*"

"Yes, Sim, and it was as hard for me to believe it at first as it is for you. You see there 's nothing expensive here; it just takes a little knack."

"I should think it took something besides 'knack,'" said Sim.

"Well, it does; it takes lots of love, the genuine

article, too, and that 's the best part. I say, Sim, you 'd better give up your 'wild West' idea; come now, won't you? You can come over here real often, and we 'll have games,— I don't mean cards, of course, but real nice games. Yes, and I 'll ask Jack over; he 's home again. You 'd better say you will, old fellow."

"It 's all right for you, Paul; but I have n't a home like this,— nor a father. I don't know as I ever wanted one before, but I feel sort of homesick to-night."

"I know how you feel, Sim; maybe you think I don't, but I do." Paul was a sympathetic, warm-hearted boy, and his sympathy did Sim good, though neither lad realized it.

After everything had been duly examined and admired, Sim took his departure, promising to come again the following Tuesday night.

"Maybe we can do a little good that way, father," suggested Mrs. Beardsley, "and I think Paul's idea, to ask the Somerville young folks over, is a good one. Of course they 're unbelievers, but we ought to try to help them all the more. Perhaps they may be won to the Lord as a result."

Mrs. Beardsley was developing a real missionary spirit, which bade fair to accomplish good work for the Master.

"Why, yes, mother, it's a first-rate idea; I would n't wonder if we could make it interesting for them, and perhaps do them some good as well."

Ethyl Somerville was naturally a kind-hearted girl, but she had been so long accustomed to having her own way that she had grown to be quite headstrong. Her one idea seemed to be to have a good time. In school she was not very studious, and often gave her teacher a deal of trouble. Yet her disposition was so sympathetic that if any of her schoolmates fell into trouble of any kind, it was Ethyl Somerville to whom they came, and into whose listening ear they poured all their sorrows; and they always went away comforted.

"Just the spirit for a good missionary," said Mrs. Blair, one day, when Minnie had been speaking of this peculiarity of Ethyl's. "Who knows into what path the Master may yet lead her young feet?" she added reflectively.

School had been closed for three or four weeks, and Emma had been very busy. She had not met

Ethyl since her return from the South, so it was arranged that Emma should call on the family, and invite Ethyl and Jack over the next Tuesday evening

It seemed to Emma that she had lived a great many years in the past few weeks. Life was broadening out before her, and she was beginning to see and feel her need of a Saviour. Not only this, but she felt a deeper anxiety for her brother than she had ever known before, although the danger of his going away from home had been so successfully averted. As she looked back over the past few months, she felt ashamed and sorry for the course she had taken, and she longed in some way to be able to counteract the wrong influence which she was sure she had exerted, especially over Ethyl Somerville; for were not her own parents Christians, while Ethyl's were unbelievers? The more she thought of it, the more anxious she became. She could hardly wait to see her friend, that she might have an opportunity of redeeming the past in some way, though she had as yet no plan of action. But it was not without many misgivings, after all, that she ran up the steps of the Somerville residence, and rang the bell.

Ethyl came to the door and seemed pleased to see her friend; but Emma noticed at once that she was looking pale and tired, and that there was a certain constraint in her manner.

"Why, Ethyl, what 's the matter? your visit has not made you sick I hope?" she asked, anxiously.

"O, no; but mother has been worse; she has been bleeding at the lungs. But she is better now, and is much stronger; the doctor says she will soon be able to ride out. We have a good nurse, but of course no one understands mama as I do, and I have been so anxious. Papa's business called him back, or we should not have returned till spring on mama's account. She can't bear to be away from him, or he would have come back alone."

"O you poor girl!" Emma exclaimed, impulsively. "I 'm so sorry for you. Mother or I ought to have been over before, but we had not heard."

"It was only last Friday that she was so bad; and as it was only a short attack, I presume but few of the neighbors knew of it. You know papa is peculiar. He has a dread of severe sickness that amounts to a perfect horror. I 've sometimes almost wondered, Emma, if he would n't be a happier man if he were not an unbeliever."

Emma was surprised and gratified. She had never seen Ethyl in any other than a careless, giddy mood, and she replied, quickly, "I have no doubt he would be, Ethyl. I think we would *all* be better and happier."

"Well, of course I don't know anything about it; but sometimes when mama is so sick, I wish I did, and I 'm sure mama feels so, too, but papa and Jack seem to have a great dislike for those 'canting Christians,' as they call them, and papa does n't like to have them even talk to mama. I 've been lonesome and tired, lately, and papa says he 'd like to have me get out more, and see if the tired look will not go away," and Ethyl sighed wearily.

"That 's just what I 'm after, so I 'm in luck," said Emma. "I came on purpose to ask you over to our house. Mother 's got my room all fixed up, and I want you to see it; and Paul wants Jack to come and see his, too. Of course you know our rooms were n't *always* pleasant, like yours," she added, blushing. "And O, Ethyl! my father and mother are converted over again. There 's as much difference in them as there is in the rooms,— though of course father and mother were always good," she declared, loyally.

"But will they let you have good times?" said Ethyl, whose curiosity was rising.

"Dear me," said Emma, "they seem more anxious than ever for me to enjoy myself, and I 'm sure I do. I 've been an awfully selfish girl, Ethyl, all my life, but I 'm going to try to do better."

"But," said Ethyl, ignoring the last remark, "they 'll not let you go to parties and dances, will they? You know you love dancing and jolly times as well as I do."

"O, no; they never *allowed* me to go to dances. I was just wicked and foolish enough to go on the sly, but I hate myself every time I think of it, I don't suppose they know it yet. It would break their hearts, I guess, if they did; but I 'm never going to do so again. I don't know but I ought to confess it to them, though."

"O, no; I guess I would n't. It would only make them feel bad," said Ethyl, whose sympathetic nature was already touched. "I suppose I ought not to have coaxed you to go."

"I 'm the most to blame, Ethyl. But you have n't promised you would come over on Tuesday evening."

"Of course I'll come, and I'll tell Jack, though I can't answer for him. You remember what your father said once on that subject." said Ethyl, with a little constraint in her manner.

"Father'll make that all right when he sees Jack. You tell him that father wishes him especially to come, and we'd all like to see him," she added, while she thought, "I hope to be able to show him that I've grown to have more sense than I once had."

When the girls parted that afternoon, they each seemed to have grown better by the visit; at least they understood each other better than ever before. Each was astonished to find in the other a depth of feeling which was before wholly unsuspected.

"I do believe," said Emma to herself, "that Ethyl is just longing to become better acquainted with the religion of Jesus. Probably she is looking to me to help her, and here I am, 'wretched, and miserable, and poor, and blind, and naked,' as father read this morning. It seems to me as if every one is better than I. It's just as Elder Blair read last Sabbath; 'The whole head is sick, and the whole heart faint.' I've been *such* a bad, ungrateful girl, it does n't seem as if I ever could hold my head up before those who have always known me, and pretend that I am forgiven. It does n't seem as if Christ could ever forgive me."

When Emma came home from her little visit, her mother was surprised to see tears in her eyes. Presently two young arms were thrown about her neck, and a trembling voice whispered in her ear: "O mother! I want to be a Christian. Won't you pray for me? I told Mrs. Blair, once, that I believed in *her* prayers, and now I believe in *yours.*"

"God bless you, my dear child! I believe I *have been praying for you every moment to-day.*"

CHAPTER VII.

A HAPPY HOME CIRCLE.

SURPRISED?—Yes; Mrs. Beardsley was surprised, so small is the faith of the human heart. She had been especially led to pray for her daughter all day, yet when the answer came, it was so sudden! Ah! we imagine it is a long way to heaven. When we write a letter to some far-away friend, we have to take distance into our calculations when looking for a reply. And too often, when we send up a prayer to the throne of glory, we think it is *so far,* or the Father is so busy answering some one else's prayers, that it will take a long time for the answer to come. And when it comes while we are "yet speaking," when Gabriel is commissioned to fly swiftly and touch us while we are still upon our knees, as he did Daniel, we are surprised. When the church prayed for Peter's deliverance, and he appeared at once, they would not believe the maid who told them. Often, truly, the answer may be years in coming; but it is not because heaven is a long way off, nor because the Father does not have bread enough and to spare, nor because he is unwilling to give it. At such times it is for us to wait in patience, believing that no good thing will be withheld.

Emma went to her room at once. It seemed to her that she must be alone. She opened her little Bible, which had grown wonderfully precious to her of late, and her eye rested upon these words: "And the Spirit and the bride say, Come. And let him that heareth say, Come. And let him that is athirst come. And whosoever will, let him take the water of life freely."

"That says 'whosoever,' and so it must mean me. Dear Lord Jesus, I can do nothing for myself; I can only *come*. Accept and forgive me because thou hast died for me, and thou hast promised."

"O mother!" she cried, seeking her mother's side. "He's promised, and I do believe him." Her only answer was an affectionate kiss; but tears of joy stood in Mrs. Beardsley's eyes, and she thought, "It seems as if I had only just begun to live."

Tuesday evening came at last. Sim Blake was the first to arrive. He was neatly dressed, and Paul and Emma were glad to notice that he came up the front steps and rang the bell, instead of going round to the back door, as on his preceding visit. Sim had never enjoyed any advantages in life, I mean in his home life. He had, however, been quite diligent in his attendance at the village school, and was no mean student. His father, naturally a kind-hearted, benevolent man, had ruined his life by strong drink, and his only son had been allowed to grow up in an atmosphere of coarseness and evil.

"We 're awful glad you 've come, Sim Blake," cried Jennie, dancing around the room.

"Come on in the parlor, and see my new jackknife father bought for me," said Jimmie.

Just then the bell rang again, and Emma went to the door to welcome Jack and Ethyl.

"Well," thought Jack, "I declare here 's Sim. I wonder what 's going to happen next!" though of course he was too well-bred to say anything but "Good-evening."

"We are very glad to see you," said Mrs. Beardsley. "Jennie, let Ethyl have this rocker, by the table."

"Jack, my boy," said the deacon, rising and extending his hand, "I owe you an apology. I 've fixed everything up with Sim, so he and I are friends now;

and I can only repeat to you what I said to him: 'My Master never forbade any one to come to see him, even if he did n't agree with his ideas in every particular. I am sorry that I so far forgot my Pattern.'"

"That 's all right, I 'm sure, deacon," said Jack, gallantly. "When Ethyl told me of your invitation, it was a question with me whether to come or not; but mother wished it, and I 'm glad I did, sir. It 's a treat to find a Christian who lives up to his profession," he added, generously.

"'Whereas I was blind, *now I see,*'" said the deacon, reverently.

"How is your mother to-night? Emma said she was not so well the other day," questioned Mrs. Beardsley.

"Mama is a little better, we think, to-day; of course she is very poorly all the time. I wish you would come and see her," said Ethyl.

"I will, and I ought to have done so before."

"How pleasant it is! I 'd no idea your rooms were so pretty and airy-looking," commented Ethyl.

"We used to keep them shut up from one year's end to another," said Paul; "*now* we use them."

Nothing I have is too good for my family," said Mrs. Beardsley, smiling on the happy-looking group.

"You are right, mother," put in the deacon; "but it took us years to learn it."

"Just see my beautiful doll, Ethyl," said Jennie, holding Miss Seraphina up for inspection. "Is n't she *mug*nificent? She 's a *brown*ett,— Emma says so. See her black eyes!"

"Yes, I see; they are perfectly visible," agreed Ethyl, whereupon Jennie hurried to her mother and said, in an audible whisper, "'Perfectly visible' means awful pretty, does n't it, mother?"

Jennie was delighted to add to her store of big words, though she was considerably disappointed when her mother explained the meaning of "visible."

After the company had listened to several early day reminiscences by both Mr. and Mrs. Beardsley, Emma inquired: "Paul, what was that puzzle in chemistry you were talking about the other day? maybe Jack can solve it. He 's pretty good in chemistry."

"Not so very," stammered Jack, glancing at Emma, who blushed as she thought: "Dear me! I hope he 's forgotten all about those silly letters. I wish *I* could.

"It 's one I saw in a paper the other day. I puzzled over it quite awhile, and I 'd like to see it done, if it can be," said Paul : "What two colorless fluids make a colored one?"

"What two colorless fluids make a colored one?" repeated Jack, reflectively.

"Maybe it 's a conundrum," suggested Sim.

"No, it is n't," said Paul: it 's a real problem; it can be done."

"O, yes," said Jack, "I m sure it can, but you will have to give me a little time. I think I can solve it."

"You shall have all the time you want," said the deacon. "I used to know a number of interesting experiments in chemistry. but that was a good many years ago. "I 'll have to brush up a little, I guess ; maybe it will make me young again, eh, mother ?"

"You will always seem young to me, father," said Mrs. Beardsley, tenderly.

"I don't s'pose you know my father used to be the *principality* of a school," piped Jennie, proudly. "I don't see why you laugh" she added, in a crest-fallen manner. "It 's true, is n't it father?"

"She means *principal,* I 'most know," corrected Jimmie.

"I simply taught a village school once," explained the deacon, "but I've almost forgotten the little I knew then."

All too soon the time came for the visitors to go. "We have had a very pleasant evening," said Ethyl, to which every one heartily assented.

"I have been thinking," said Mrs. Beardsley, "how nice it would be for you all to come three weeks from to-night, and we will form a little society for mutual improvement, and try to meet on the first Tuesday in every month this winter."

"O yes! do!" cried Emma and Paul at once "and let's all be thinking what we shall name it, till we meet again."

"Agreed," said Jack, "and meanwhile I'll try to study out that question in chemistry."

"You'll come, of course, Sim?" asked Paul.

"O, I don't know; I can't promise," said Sim, who did not care much about the prospect of spending a whole evening solving knotty questions in chemistry.

"O, I know! Sim's strong point is mathematics," said Ethyl, knowingly. "If we have a touch of that in the program, he'll come, I know he will."

"I'll tell you," said Paul; "let Sim give us a hard

problem next time, and we will rack our brains on it."

"Well, I'll see," said Sim doubtfully, as, with a cheery "good night," the little party broke up.

When Sim reached his lonely home that night, the contrast was so great between it and Paul's pleasant one, that he fell to musing: "Well, if Christianity makes things pleasant like that, and folks nice and kind, I wish there was a little of it in *this* home; but there 's no use talking; there never will be, and I 'm going to leave. Paul won't go with me, that 's sure," he reflected, as he crept into bed. "You 're alone in this world, Sim Blake, and have been ever since mother died," and something very like a tear trickled down the boy's cheek, and fell on the dingy pillow. He lay awake that night until his plans were fully matured. Meanwhile, he heard his father enter, and with a heavy, unsteady step, seek his bed.

"I wonder if *he 'll* care when he finds I 've skipped. I don't believe he will," and the lonely boy fell into an uneasy slumber, from which the rays of the morning sun, streaming into his eyes from a little window at the foot of his bed, awoke him. Sim had not intended to go until the next month; but he and his father had had a wretched quarrel the day before, and now he decided not to wait even as long as he had at first planned.

"There 's no use talking. I just can't stand it another day, *and I won't,*" he declared, bitterly. "I 'll go this very night; nobody 'll care, anyway. I 'm sure father 'll be glad, and as for grandmother, she said to-day she wished I 'd go off somewhere, and never come back,— and I will. I 'll take the midnight train for Chicago. If I had a home like Paul's I would n't mind settling down; but I have n't; so here goes." And the miserable boy set about making his few preparations.

He went to bed early that night; but slept only a little. Eleven o'clock came at last. He had slept with his clothes on, and his little bundle was ready at the head of his bed. He took only a few cookies from a pan in the cupboard, and a drink of water as he passed the pail. He wondered if grandmother would miss the cookies in the morning, and scold. He could hear his father's heavy breathing from the next room, and he felt a strong desire to look on his face once more, so he turned the lamp down low, and softly entered the room.

"No, there 's no use; I don't care to see him again, nor he me," and he turned to go. "Yes, I *must* look on his face again — *just once.*"

The dim light fell on a purple, bloated face; but it did not waken the sleeper, who was wrapped in a profound, drunken slumber. The lonely boy shuddered, glanced around once more at the familiar objects, and opened the door.

"Wait! I 'll take mother's picture; it 's all I 've got on earth. I 'll have it."

Softly he re-entered the dimly lighted room, secured his treasure, and went out into the night,— aye, went out, as many another boy has done before; miserable, almost hopeless, without money, without friends, *without love,* another victim to the curse of strong drink. Out into the night he went, hedged about by no mother's prayers, no sister's love, no father's blessing — out into the night — the dreary night. But the night of sin and shame and suffering into which he is entering is blacker still. Will no friendly voice reach him from the darkness? Where is the hand of love that will clasp his, and lead him upward? Is there none? God pity him! he is gone — and alone — out into the night.

"Yes,—I Must Look on His Face Again."

CHAPTER VIII.

TEMPTED AND TRIED.

YOU and I, dear reader, will not attempt to follow the poor wanderer in his travels,— from Chicago to Kansas, then still farther west, where, on the broad prairies, he led the reckless life of a cowboy. But the angels, the ministering spirits of heaven, did not leave him. God and the angels follow many a poor human soul long after he has been given up and left to perish by his fellow men.

Let us return to the deserted home, and take a peep at its inmates. It is the next evening after Sim's departure, and Grandmother Blake has just prepared the evening meal. She sits silently and tearfully sipping her tea, which she holds with a trembling hand to her lips. Mr. Blake, or "Old Pete," as he is familiarly known in the village, is eating his supper in sullen silence.

"I tell ye, Pete, that boy 's gone fer good, and these old eyes 'll never see 'im no more," she wailed.

"Well, let him go; he ain't no good here," was the

surly response; "there 'll be one less mouth to feed."

"Yes, Peter; an' there 'll be another less before many days. I feel it and know it. O, ef only I 'd been better to Sim, I could die easy. Do you s'pose I 'll ever see 'im agin, Pete? What made me so cross to the boy?—I dunno. I had a feelin' fer 'im all the time? but I never let 'im know,—*I never let 'im know,*"—she repeated, drearily.

Ah, too many of us are like Grandmother Blake. We do not let our dear ones know how we love them. May we never have to repeat, with aching hearts, when it is too late, the sad refrain, "I never let them know!"

"O, he 'll be back 'fore long, never you fear," growled the boy's father.

"Never, Peter; never while I live;" and the old woman's firm assurance seemed afterward almost like a prophecy.

The next day, as Paul was going to the village on an errand, Jack hailed him. "Hallo, Paul! Sim's gone for good, they say. Just saw Old Pete around the corner. Guess you 'll be out one, in the next meeting of dignitaries at your house."

"Whew!" whistled Paul. "Well, I must say I

sort of thought that fellow would back out of that Western scheme yet. I tried my best to get him to."

"You know you *did* intend to go with him, one spell," said Jack, with a provoking smile.

"I know I did; but you know, Jack, there 's been a great change over at our house, in more ways than one."

"Yes, yes; deacon s real sociable; but say, Paul what 's come over Em? she does n't act a bit as she used to."

"She 's getting to be a lot more sensible and womanly, I know that; and *I* think she 's been converted."

"Well, there 's an end to good times, if she has," said Jack, sneeringly.

"Don't say that, Jack; did n't we have a jolly time the other night?" said Paul, loyally.

"O yes, very good. But come on, Paul; we have n't had a game of euchre nor a good cigar together, in a long time. Come, let 's go into Brown's and get the cigars."

Paul was undecided, and he hesitated just a moment. He had made up his mind never to smoke another cigar, and he felt miserable, already, to think he had broken his word to his sister; but that moment's hesitation gave the enemy a chance to whisper in his ear, "Jack will be offended; he'll think you are no gentleman."

"Come, Paul, hurry up," urged Jack. "What's the matter? You're not getting pious, too, I hope? I declare, I'd no idea you *were* such a baby," he sneered.

That was too much for Paul. He could endure anything better than ridicule.

"Who's refused, Jack Somerville? *I* have n't, he cried, his face the color of scarlet; and with great bravado he stepped up to the smiling clerk, and bought half a dozen cigars. Then he and Jack each lighted one, with an air of great complacency.

But Paul had never felt so mean in his life. He kept thinking of the many kindnesses his parents and sister had shown him of late, and more than all, of his broken promise, and he was so uncomfortable that Jack found him a poor companion. When the boys parted that afternoon, Jack wondered what had come over Paul, while Paul himself hurried home with a better understanding of how Judas must have felt than he ever wanted to have again. He almost decided to own up the whole miserable business to Emma, and tell Jack, on the next Tuesday night, that he was done with that sort of thing; but when he reached home, someway he did n't have the courage, and he ate his supper in silence.

Emma rallied him a little on his absent-mindness, and what ordinarily would not have vexed him at all irritated him wonderfully in his present mood. "Can't a fellow be let alone a minute?" he cried, and spitefully throwing his cap on the table, he hurried up to his room.

"What 's the matter with Paul?" said Emma, sighing deeply. Ah, the blessed Spirit had been striving with him, and the enemy was determined not to give him up. That night, when Emma knelt by her bed in the little room already associated with tender memories of past prayers and past blessings, there went up to the loving Father a more earnest petition than ever before for her brother; for she felt that a critical moment had come in his life, and that he was in danger.

Paul was sure he could hear her sobbing in her room. "I am a selfish bear," he muttered. "I 'll own up in the morning — Sabbath morning — I surely will."

"Let 's kiss and make up, Em," said he, the moment he could catch her alone the next morning. "I 'm sorry I was so wolfish to you. Yes,"— as Emma turned her face away, while a pained expression flitted over it,—"yes, I knew you 'd smell that cigar. I 'm going to own up, and quit, if it does make Jack mad. I don't enjoy this sort of thing as I used to, and I 'm going to tell him so; — besides, I 've lied to you."

"O Paul!" and two loving arms were around his neck, while the hot tears fell like rain. "I just knew there was something the matter; and, O, I 've been praying for you, and dreaming about you all night."

"Well, never mind, sis; this ends it. I 'm going to behave myself after this. I hate myself every time I think of cigars or euchre, either. When father and mother and you have done so much for me, I ought to be the best fellow in the world. I 'm glad I did n't go with Sim, poor boy!"

"I can not thank God enough. But, O Paul, you can never do right in your own strength. I 've tried it, and failed more than once. God will help you, if you want him to; ask him Paul."

All that Sabbath day the words kept ringing in his ears, "God will help you; ask him, Paul." All nature seemed to be pleading with him. The ticking of the old-fashioned clock in the sitting-room, that used to be Grandmother Beardsley's, seemed to say, "Ask him, ask him!" and the gentle murmur of the wind through the tall pines in the front yard echoed it plainly, "Ask him, Paul, ask him!"

O Paul, the blessed Spirit is striving with you mightily, and you are even now hearing the same Voice that, on the road to Damascus, spoke to your illustrious namesake: "Why persecutest thou me? . . It is hard for thee to kick against the pricks."

Mrs. Beardsley found time the next Monday afternoon to call on Mrs. Somerville. She found the invalid very poorly indeed. Mrs. Beardsley was much pleased that her hostess turned the conversation at once upon religious subjects.

"My parents were Christians, and if they had only lived, it might have been so different. But they both died before my marriage; and you know, Mrs. Beardsley, how hard it would naturally be for me to live up to my early teachings under the circumstances, though a better husband than mine never lived, nor a kinder one," she added, loyally.

"I dare say Captain Somerville has been watching

professed Christians, and sees so many inconsistencies in their lives that he has persuaded himself that religion is all false. O, I fear my own life has been one long period of scattering instead of gathering with the Master," said Mrs. Beardsley, sadly. "But he is the only pattern; we have only one, though it is very sad that the lives of his professed followers are often unworthy of imitation."

"I have sometimes wondered why God should permit his children,— for I suppose we are all his by right of creation,— to suffer so, if he loves them. I 'm sure it gives me no pleasure to see my children suffer," sighed Mrs. Somerville.

"It is not for his pleasure, but for our good, so that the dross will all be burned away. The Bible says he sits as a refiner of silver, and watches the burning of the dross, until he can see reflected in us his divine image. He *sits.* He will not leave our side for a moment. 'Lo, I am with you alway,' is his sweet assurance, and he says he doth not willingly afflict nor grieve the children of men."

Mrs. Somerville was weeping quietly now; but in a moment her face lighted up with an expression of hope and confidence, that her visitor had never seen there before, and as she rose to go, Mrs. Somerville said earnestly,—

"You have done me good, Mrs. Beardsley; will you come again? and O, my friend, will you pray for me? and — and — yes, will you pray for *my husband?*"

"I will; God will help you. He is so willing to receive you," she answered.

When Mrs. Beardsley reached home that day, there was a psalm of thanksgiving upon her lips. Emma met her at the door.

"O mother!" she said, "I have seen Minnie Blair. It seems such a long time since I saw her last; I 'm glad school will begin again soon. They had heard of Sim's going away, and she came for particulars. They feel so sad about it; and, O mother! are n't you glad? Minnie 's coming over to our next meeting, and has promised, if her parents are willing, to join our circle. Paul and I can go 'most home with her, you know. She is such a Bible student and so good in history, that it will be nice; for of course we 'll have a little Bible study with the rest; do n't you think that would be a good plan?"

"Your idea is most excellent, my daughter. Your father will be highly pleased, I know. Yes, I 'm glad

Minnie is coming, for I am quite sure of her parents' consent. But, what is it, Emma? what is it? Were you going to tell me tomething else, child?"

"I want to tell you — O, I must tell you, mother — Paul is growing to be a different boy. Of course you know that; but he told me to-day that he *wished he were a Christian,* and I am sure God is hearing our prayers."

Mrs. Beardsley put her arm around her daughter, and wept for very joy. Just then the deacon came in from the barn. "Well, mother?" he said questioningly.

"Emma says the good Spirit is striving with Paul, father; the Lord is answering our prayers; but what small faith we have had!"

"Yes, mother; little faith indeed; but whereas I was blind, now I see. Here I am, Lord, and the children whom thou hast given me. Bless the Lord, O my soul; praise ye the Lord."

CHAPTER IX.

ENTERTAINMENTS AT HOME.

"GOOD evening, Minnie; I see that our friends have begun to arrive; and I 'm so glad you could come!" cried Emma heartily.

"Well, you are not alone in being glad," said Paul, gallantly.

"There seems to be a suggestion of snow in the air this evening; but I dare say you young folks do n't mind that. Come, have a seat by the fire. I suppose you have something very instructive and interesting for our little circle to-night, Miss Minnie," said the deacon.

"This is my first night, you know, and I did n't think that much would be asked of me."

"It 's the first night with all of us; that is, we have n't anything arranged for work yet," said Emma.

Just then Jack and Ethyl arrived, and after they had been heartily welcomed by all, the deacon was elected chairman, and the meeting was declared open.

"What shall be the name of this august assemblage?" demanded the chairman, with a merry smile.

"I suppose we are all members?" queried Ethyl.

"Yes," piped Jennie, "cause father said we'd all be *carter* members."

Poor Jennie was a little disturbed by the laugh which followed; but, as usual, Jimmie came to her rescue.

"Never mind, Jennie; I would n't feel bad one bit. Father said charter members, but *I* do n't know what he meant."

"Who will explain it?" the deacon asked.

"Well, Jennie, my girl, a charter member is one of the very first members of any society or organization."

"I have been thinking of calling ours the Happy Home Circle," said Minnie.

"That's just the thing,— so suggestive," said Jack.

"'Course 't is," agreed Jennie, who had already recovered her composure.

At last, after some discussion, it was agreed to accept the suggested name, and the Happy Home Circle started out on its career in an earnest search for knowledge.

"I suppose Jack is prepared to solve that problem in chemistry. If so, we are ready to hear and applaud," said Paul.

"Please do n't applaud until we see whether the thing works," said Jack, producing, from an inside pocket, two bottles. "Now if you will bring me two glasses of water, Jennie, we will proceed with our experiment."

Jennie soon returned with the glasses, and Jack then put a few drops of prussiate of potash into one glass of water, and into the other a little weak solution of sulphate of iron in water.

"There," said Jack, "you see these mixtures are colorless; but now let us pour them together." He did so; and held up to the astonished gaze of his admiring audience a tumberful of blue fluid.

"Bravo!" cried the deacon. "Why, Jack, you are a regular magician."

"You ought to be a great professor," said Mrs. Beardsley.

"I have been thinking that I would so like to know what process Moses used when he dissolved the golden calf in water, and made the Israelites drink of it," said Minnie Blair, whose inclinations toward Biblical literature were very marked.

"Why would n't that be a good question to study on through the week?" queried Paul.

"I suppose it can be done all right," said Jack, "though I had no idea that Moses understood the art, away back there."

"Moses, you know, was learned in all the wisdom of the Egyptians, and they were at that time the most learned people on the face of the earth," said the deacon.

"I do n't know much about Bible history, as I presume you have guessed," laughed Jack. "To me the Bible is a book of unreasonable stories and absurd contradictions."

"I 'll tell you," said Minnie; "it 's because Jack does n't understand it. Now suppose he brings a few of his theological puzzles into our next meeting. Then we can see if we are as skillful in explaining them as he has been in demonstrating to us his ability in chemistry."

"Agreed," said Jack; "but I did not finish my chemical experiments. Jennie, you just get me two more glasses, please, and we will have still another color for you, made from two colorless liquids."

Jennie ran for the glasses, proud that she could be of use; and Jack again poured a few drops of prussiate of potash into one glass of water, and a little nitrate of bismuth into the other. He then quickly poured the contents of the two together, and the result was a bright yellow liquid.

"Well," said the deacon, "you are really doing well."

"Now, if I should add to a solution of prussiate of potash that of sulphate of copper, I would have a reddish brown fluid, from two colorless ones."

"Well, Jimmie, I suppose you and Jennie would like something that you can do. These other things are pretty hard for you," said Mrs. Beardsley.

"O, yes, mother!" eagerly assented Jimmie, "We 'd like to be members of the circle, would n't we Jennie?"

"'Course we would, Jimmie Beardsley!"

"Well, bring me a piece of thread, a button, and a little salt. That 's right. Now, I shall add a drop of water to the salt held in my hand, and very thoroughly wet the thread in it. I will now tie this little button to one end of it, and hang it up a moment to dry — so. Now, Jennie, please bring me a match, and I 'll show you a strange sight."

By this time the string was dry, and quite easily ignited by holding the lighted match under it. When the thread was all burned, what was the surprise of the twins to see that the button still remained, suspended in the air by a thread of ashes, which had been so toughened by the salt that it readily held the weight of the button.

After a pleasant visit it was thought best to adjourn; and as the interest seemed to demand it, it was decided to meet again the next week.

* * * * *

When all were again seated around the large center-table in Deacon Beardsley's pleasant sitting-room, the next Tuesday evening, Emma introduced her friend Polly Brown and her brother Will, whom she felt sure they would all gladly welcome. It was decided also to extend a cordial invitation to Elder Blair and his wife to drop in on any evening when they could spare the time. The chairman then asked Jack if he was prepared with those Biblical questions of which he wished an explanation.

"Well, I 'll tell you, deacon. I suppose you think I am going to ask how the whale could swallow Jonah, or how God could create the world in six literal days, or something of the kind, but I am not. I 've read the account of the whale miracle since last Tuesday night; for I *did* intend to bring that up, having always been told that the whale has a very small throat. But in reading the account, I was surprised to notice that the word 'whale' is not in the story; so you see I understand that now without any asking."

"Let me explain, Jack," replied the deacon, "that the word 'whale' is used in the New Testament, in relating the narrative; but you remember that while one kind of whale has a small throat, there is another kind which has a large one."

"Sure enough, deacon; I believe you are right," said Jack.

"Well, now, that 's good," said Minnie. "If you 'd read your Bible real carefully, Jack, I would n't wonder if you could answer a great many of the questions that now puzzle you."

"Perhaps I could; but there 's one question which I do n't believe can ever be made plain to me. The Bible says, 'God is love,' and 'his mercy endureth forever,' and lots of such things; and vet Christians believe that when any one dies, if he has not faith in Christ, he must burn forever and ever in the most awful torment, just for a short life of sin here."

"Dear me!" said Jennie, shuddering, "It can't be *our* Lord he 's talking about."

"'Course not," whispered Jimmie, decisively.

"I do not wonder this troubles you, Jack; it did me until I learned that the Bible teaches nothing of the kind," said the deacon, smiling.

"Why, Deacon Beardsley!" It was Jack's turn to be astonished now. "I thought everybody that was a Christian believed that."

"I am sure it would be better for you to study it out for yourself, so I will simply give you a few texts for reference;" and Jack took out his note-book and wrote:—

Mal. 4:1-4; Ps. 37:10, 20, 36; 104:35.

"Give him Rom. 6:23," suggested Minnie.

"That is a good one," said the deacon. "Now perhaps this will do for one study."

"Did any one find how the golden calf could be so mixed with water that one could drink it?" asked Paul.

"I did not find it," said Jack. "Maybe it would be better to ask the chairman how it is done."

"Well," said the deacon, "we might first form chlorid of gold from the solid gold, which can be done by putting it into nitric acid and water, and applying heat. Then if this is put into water, it will quite readily dissolve and unite with it."

"I 'll have to try that sometime, I think," said Jack, to whom anything which related to chemistry was interesting.

Jimmie sat by the table holding in his chubby hand a long tube. "What have you there, Jimmie?" asked Will Brown.

"It 's Paul's kaleidoscope," said Jimmie, handing it to him.

"O is n't it funny! How regular all those diamonds look! and it changes every time I move it. Just see it, Polly," cried Will. "It 's just like Cousin Katie's. Uncle made hers, but I do n't see how he did it."

"Paul made this," cried Jennie, boastfully. "He 's a regular *genesis!*"

"Genius," corrected Mrs. Beardsley, smiling.

"It 's very easily done," said Paul. "Take three pieces of glass about an inch and a half wide by six or seven in length, which you can cut with a glazier's diamond. Pieces of looking-glass are the best; but any window glass will do if you paint the outside black; then take a few bits of beads and tiny pieces of glass of all colors, and put inside; put little glass windows at each end of the three-cornered tube which you now have made, enclose it in a round piece of pasteboard, cover the ends with paper, having a hole in it as large as a five-cent piece; the end you intend to look through should be the smaller. Then cover the whole with anything you like. Emma covered this one with blue plush, which makes a very pretty little instrument," said Paul, holding it up daintily.

"O, we 'll have one!" cried Polly, joyfully, "for I know you can make one, can't you, Will?"

"O, yes, I think so," answered her brother.

The young people then spent some time in singing, and all were surprised to see that the evening had passed away so quickly, and that it was time to separate.

"My!" soliloquized Paul, "I don't see what fun

there ever was in sneaking away from home nights. Poor Sim! I wonder where he is now."

Ah, Paul, could you see the poor wanderer as the pitying angels of God see him, you would weep tears of sorrow.

Polly and Will Brown were delighted to find a bright spot in their usually monotonous life, and Jack Somerville actually admitted to himself that he had spent three very pleasant evenings at the deacon's, and went to sleep wondering what those Bible texts would prove.

"Well," said Mrs. Beardsley, "we have got Jack Somerville to studying the Bible, anyway; who knows what may come of it?"

Deacon Beardsley smiled, and again repeated his favorite text of Scripture: "Whereas I was blind, now I see."

* * * * *

The time for the Circle has again arrived.

"You did n't have much to do at our last circle," said the deacon, addressing the twins, as they stood side by side.

"No; we did n't, did we, Jimmie?" asked Jennie, with a grieved, sidewise glance at her brother.

"Never mind, Jennie; maybe they'll let us do something to-night."

"I'll tell you a story, if you'll bring me a string," said the deacon, "and maybe I can finish it before the company comes."

Jennie quickly brought a piece of common wrapping-twine, about a yard long, which the deacon pronounced just the thing. He then tied the ends together, the twins watching every movement with eager eyes.

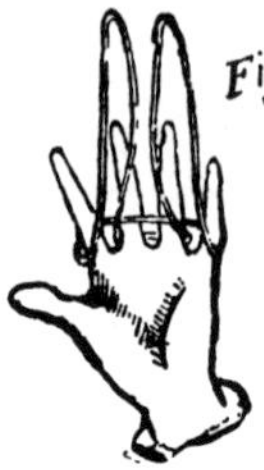

"Now," said the deacon, holding his left hand with the palm up, and letting the string fall over the palm, "you see just how I am fixing this string." Then he spread his fingers and brought forward the loops which hung behind, then loosened the loop, and took hold of the string that crossed his hand, and drew it forward. He next put his forefinger and little finger under the string that encircled the same fingers of the other hand, and passed the two loops to the back of his hand, as shown in Fig. 1. He then tucked both loops under the cross-strings at the back, and began his story, while Jimmie's eyes sparkled with excitement, and Jennie whispered, " Is n't this fun, Jimmie Beardsley? and is n't our father lovely? "

" Once upon a time," said the deacon, " there was an old man who wanted some candles so much that he stole a whole pound of them; see! here they are." He then hooked his forefinger under the cross-piece at the back, and drew it down till it could be passed over the second and third fingers to the front. He then passed it over, and drew it slowly upward, as shown in Fig. 2.

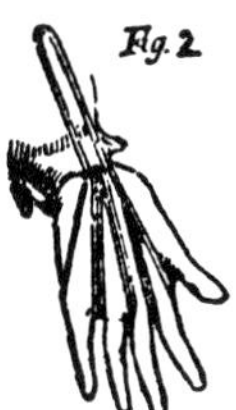

" There they are, Jennie! don't you remember how the candles looked that mother had once? " said Jimmie.

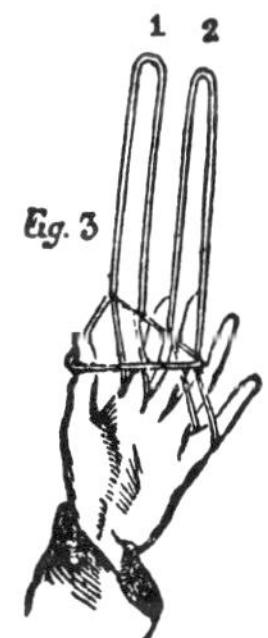

1. Right forefinger.
2. Right middle finger.

" The old man was tired, and as soon as he got his stolen candles home, he hung them up, so " (hanging the long loop over the thumb). " Then he sat down to rest in his chair, which had a high back. This is the very chair," said the deacon, laughing at the growing excitement of the twins. Quickly hitching the right forefinger and middle finger under the loops which were hanging behind the left hand, and bringing them in front, he raised them perpendicularly, when there was the chair plain enough. This is shown in Fig. 3. "Well, when the old man had rested himself, in his high-backed chair, long enough, he took these scissors to cut down a candle for himself to use.

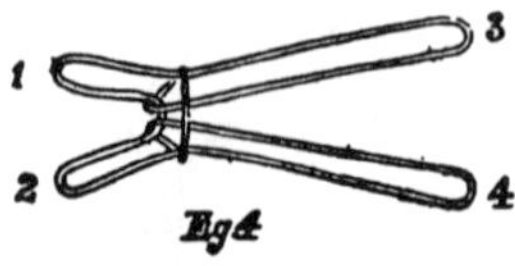

1. Forefinger of left hand.
2. Little finger of left hand.
3. Forefinger of right hand.
4. Middle finger of right hand.

See; here are the scissors." As he said this, he quickly slipped the loop off his thumb, and moved the blades and handles of the scissors, as if he were cutting something (Fig. 4), while the twins shouted with laughter.

"Just as he had got his candle lighted, a policeman, who had been sent to arrest him for stealing the candles, came in and produced his staff, which had the queen's crown on top of it. Here it is," he said, letting go the little finger of his left hand, when the loop ran up the string toward the right hand, and there was the crown-topped staff. This is shown in Fig. 5. "The old man was bound not to be taken; but the policeman called for help, and then

1. Right middle finger.
2. Right forefinger.

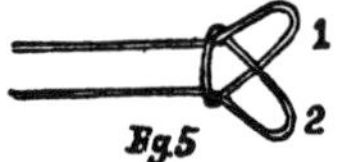

1. Right forefinger.
2. Left hand.

tied the old man's arms, like this," continued the deacon, slipping the right middle finger out of its loop, "and carried the poor old thief off to prison." Fig. 6.

Of course the twins were delighted, and the deacon whispered to his wife, while Emma ran to open the door to admit their friends: "Strange I never thought to do anything to amuse those little tots before! Did you see how pleased they were? Well, Whereas I was blind, *now* I see," and the deacon arose and heartily welcomed the young folks.

Fig. 7

"Father's been telling Jimmie and me just the nicest story," said Jennie, with enthusiasm; and she would not rest until the deacon had repeated it for the company.

"Mother has an egg puzzle," said Emma, "and it 's a pretty cute one; show us how it is done, mother."

"Well, bring me an egg and two small glasses, please, Jennie," said Mrs. Beardsley.

When these were brought, she placed the egg in the glass, as shown in Fig. 7, and said, "You see about half the egg is above the glass rim, and that there is about an eighth of an inch between the edge of the rim and the egg. Now do you think it would be possible to take the egg out of the glass, and put it into the glass beside it, without touching either glass or egg? Who can do it?"

"Well," said Jack, "really, that 's a little out of my line. It 's worse than the puzzle in chemistry."

"I don't think *I* could do it," said Minnie Blair, "and I don't see how *you* can."

"I am quite sure the transfer can be made easily," said Mrs. Beardsley, "simply by calling to my aid the help of one of the greatest forces of nature — the air."

She then smilingly bent over, and blew hard upon the side of the egg farthest from the empty glass, when, sure enough, the pressure pushed the egg completely over into the other glass.

"You see," said Mrs. Beardsley, "the air-pressure is considerable at the bottom of the glass, and is enough to force the egg from its resting-place."

"Well, that 's queer," said Ethyl.

"Now," said Minnie Blair, "I 'll just show you something, seeing you have the egg and glass so handy. Have you a spoonful of alcohol in the house?"

"There 's a trifle left from the camphor," said Emma.

"I just want to show you what alcohol will do in the human stomach,—the effect is dreadful," said Minnie; and taking the bottle and pouring a little of the contents into the empty glass, she broke the egg into it.

"My! Jimmie Beardsley! just see that egg get white!" cried Jennie excitedly.

"It 's cooking it," said Jack. "I had heard somewhere that alcohol would do that, but I never believed it till now."

"Well, does n't that beat all?" said Ethyl. "You are so scientific, Minnie."

"Oh, I 've seen papa do that when he gives a lecture on temperance."

"Just think," observed the deacon. "what alcohol must do in the human stomach."

"Why, I just believe it cooks that, too," said Jimmie.

"Course it does, Jimmie Beardsley, and we must n't ever taste it," said Jennie, solemnly shaking her head.

"That 's right," said Minnie; "if you only stick to that, you 'll never die a drunkard."

"Now," said Paul, "I believe we 'll try another experiment before those glasses are put away; but a tumbler is better,— that 's right Jennie. Now if father will lend me two half-dollars,— I guess I have a ten-cent piece,— I 'll show you the trick."

The two half-dollars and the dime were produced, and upon the large coins, Paul set the goblet, placing the small coin between the others, as you see in the illustration.

" Now, my scientific friends," said he, " will you get that ten-cent piece for me without touching either coins or glass? "

Fig. 1

" It can't be done! course not! " gravely decided Jennie.

" It looks like a pretty hard case," said Jack.

" Do you all give it up? " asked Paul, when they had each examined the coins and the goblet to their satisfaction.

" Yes, I guess we 'll have to," said Polly Brown.

" Well, it 's a very simple thing to do. I have only to say the word, so to speak, and the coin comes traveling my way, fast enough," and Paul, assuming a very mysterious air, slowly repeated these words, while he scratched the tablecloth with his nail, in the direction in which he wished to make the ten-cent piece move: —

> " 'Little dime, do not stay
> In a place so out of the way;
> But when my finger moved shall be,
> Like a good fellow, come to me!' "

And, sure enough, the little coin, with a slow, gliding movement, left its position under the glass, and crept straight toward Paul's hand.

"Well, well, young man," said the deacon, laughing, "I 'd like to know where you learned that caper."

"It is one I read about; I 've been saving it up for to-night, you see."

The twins were wild with delight by this time, and every one was pleased with the experiment.

"Say, Paul, what made it do that way? can't you tell me?" said Jimmie, who always wanted a reason for everything.

"Why, little brother, don't you see that it was the vibration — the jarring motion of the tablecloth — that made it move?"

"Course," commented Jennie wisely, "course, Jimmie Beardsley, it was the *bi-bi-bi-ver-ation!*"

"Now, since you have had already one illustration of the force of air-pressure, I guess we will have another example," said the deacon. "I used to be able to do it, if I 've not lost my knack." Saying which, he took one of the small glasses, placed the dime in the bottom, dropping a twenty-five-cent piece over it, as shown in Fig. 2.

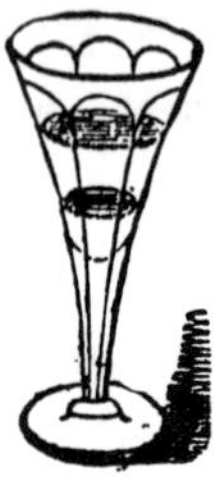

Fig. 2

"Now, then, I wonder if that ten-cent piece can be got out of that glass without touching either the glass or the coins," he said.

"Dear me," said Will Brown, laughing. "I am prepared for almost anything mysterious now; I dare say it can be, though I don't see how."

"Well, suppose I show you," said the deacon, as he blew a quick, hard puff down the side of the glass. In a moment the larger coin turned up on its side, and the ten-cent piece came flying over the top of the glass.

Of course every one laughed, and the deacon said: "That 's an old-fashioned game. But what do you think people fifty years ago would have thought of the things we see every day — the wonders of electricity, the steam-cars, and a thousand and one other things?"

"Yes, father," said Mrs. Beardsley. "The young

folks would n't know how to live now-a-days with the clumsy conveniences we used to be obliged to work with. Just tell them about the log chimneys and the clay ovens your people used when you were a boy."

"O, yes, do!" echoed a half-dozen voices.

"When I was a boy," said the deacon, smiling, and drawing his chair a little nearer the fire, "I often watched my father while he made the family bake-oven. He would first make a platform of boards, and cover it with clay; then, bending hoop-poles in the shape he wanted his oven, he would put boards or bark over them, and fasten them to the platform securely enough to hold up the mud, which he spread carefully over the entire structure, leaving a small opening in the back part, and a door in front. Then he would light a fire on the inside, to burn out the boards, poles, etc., and dry the mud. Then the oven was ready to use.

"When I was a boy and lived in the woods, very poor people used to build fires against the side of the house, leaving a hole in the roof for the smoke to escape. When the backlog would burn out, they would pull it forward, and put in another. Sometimes the house itself would catch fire, and then, ——'

"What did they do then?" asked Jennie, whose eyes were growing very large.

"O, it didn't worry them much. One night a neighbor's house caught fire in this way, and one of the girls called her brother, very slowly and deliberately, 'Al-bert! Al-bert! get up, and put out the house: it's all afire!'

"Albert did not hear the first time she called, nor the second, but Melissa was patient,—the logs were wet and green, and she knew there was time enough. So she kept on calling until the brother responded, and, constituting himself a fire department, subdued the flames."

"I don't believe the old-fashioned fire was as hot as fires are now," laughed Jack.

And now the little company, thanking the deacon for his story, took their departure.

CHAPTER X.

A TARDY REPENTANCE.

THE Beardsley family were seated in the dining-room at the breakfast table next morning, when a timid knock was heard at the kitchen door.

"I wonder who's there; you run and open the door, Jennie," said Emma.

In a moment, Jennie appeared, followed by a ragged little boy of about her own age, who stood a moment in embarrassed silence, holding a dirty cap in one hand, and cramming the other, blue with cold, as far into his pocket as he could.

"It's Jet Burns," explained Jimmie; "sometimes he goes to school in my room."

"Yes, I'm Jet Burns," assented the little traveler, wiping his nose on his sleeve, and edging up toward the fire.

"Well, what can I do for you, Jet?" asked Mrs. Beardsley, mentally wondering if any one in the world ever had done anything for him.

"Nuthin', fur me," piped the dismal little voice;

"but, say, Mis' Beardsley, ole Pete, he tole me to come an' tell ye the ole woman was a sinkin', an' wants ter see ye."

"Is that so! well, of course I'll go. Can you manage the dishes, daughter? you'll be late to school, but ——"

"Yes, I'm Jet Burns."

"Why, yes, of course, mother. Poor old soul! She will probably die. I've heard she takes Sim's going away very much to heart," said Emma.

While Mrs. Beardsley packed a basket of food, which she knew would be needed, Emma interested herself in the little messenger.

"Where do you live, Jet? Here, take this cooky; you look hungry."

"Thankee, ma'am, I be," assented Jet. "I live

in that there little house clost to ole Pete's; we ain't lived there not so very long. My! this here cooky 's good! have 'em *every day?*"

"Why, the child is really hungry," said the deacon. "Here, Jet, have another, and put these in your pocket; wrap them up for him, Emma. I did n't know there was such a family in town,— but I *ought* to have known;" and something very like a tear glistened in the deacon's eye, and the single word "*Inasmuch*" fell from his trembling lips.

Jet trotted along by Mrs. Beardsley's side, much elated that he had been the bearer of such important news; and then — those cookies! What *would* Tot say! Tot was his youngest and favorite sister. The anticipation was too much for Jet, and he bounded away, leaving Mrs. Beardsley thoroughly astonished that *such* a waif should have lived in Jonesville, and she never have known it. After some trouble, she lifted aside the rickety gate, and knocked softly at the front door.

"Come in," said a gruff voice, which announced the fact that the old man was at home. Mrs. Beardsley found the aged invalid propped up in bed, moaning piteously, and calling for Sim constantly, while her rough nurse was urging her to eat, with gruff kindness, some hot gruel he had been making.

"She seems to be out of her head, Mr. Blake," said Mrs. Beardsley, slipping on a large apron and rolling up her sleeves.

"Yes, ma'am; she ain't been right ever sence that boy run away. I'd no idee she sot sech store by him."

"Do you hear anything from him?"

"O, no: I hain't the least idee where he 's gone to. Course 't aint no great shakes of a home,— ourn ain't,— but then, it 's a home. That boy allus *was* an ongrateful critter."

"Poor boy! I 'm *so* sorry!"

Hour after hour passed, and still Mrs. Beardsley tarried to minister to the dying woman, of whose recovery good Dr. Willis gave no hope. Jet Burns was glad to run over again to the deacon's, at noon, with news from the invalid, and with word that Mrs. Beardsley would not be home till evening. All day long she listened to the feeble moaning of the invalid, and her pitiful calls for Sim: "O Sim! if you 'll only come 'long back, granny 'll be good to ye. *Come, Sim!* Pete won't lick ye no more, I know he won't,— I won't let him. I 'd orter brung ye up better 'n I did yer father. I will next time, Sim,— *next time.* Granny 'll get a good supper, Sim; here 's some more cookies — you allus liked cookies."

Just as the great red sun was going down in the west, Grandmother Blake opened her eyes for a moment,—eyes that were already dimmed by the breath of the pale Visitor,—and called Mrs. Beardsley to her side.

"My race is e'en a'most run,— it 's Mis' Beardsley, ain't it?" she said. "I did n't never know ye very well, but Sim uster speak o' your folks; an', O Mis' Beardsley, you 'll see him *sometime!* He 'll come back sometime, an' won't ye tell him granny wanted ter see him 'fore she died? *won't ye?* O, I loved the boy, Mis' Beardsley,— I loved him, but I did n't let him know,— *did n't let him know.* Good-by, Pete; hope ye 'll see yer way clear to quit drinkin'; I was allus sot agin' it, Pete."

The words were so low now as scarcely to be heard. The breath grew fainter and shorter. Mrs. Beardsley tried to speak of the Christian's hope and the love of Christ, but the ears were deaf to the voice of love and pity. The poor conscience-stricken sufferer was at rest.

Old Pete managed to keep comparatively sober until

after the funeral, when he relapsed into a worse condition than before. The last restraint was gone now, and he had no one left to remonstrate, no matter how feebly, with him.

The next Sabbath after the funeral, Elder Blair preached to an attentive audience, from the impressive words: "Go out into the highways and hedges, and compel them to come in." Many were deeply impressed that they had a duty to do in this direction, and, as on a previous occasion so well remembered by them, Deacon Beardsley and his wife were sensibly moved.

The deacon determined that he would try to better the condition of the Burns family, of whom poor Jet was the only member he had as yet seen. Mrs. Beardsley and Emma were impressed to do something to lift up and help poor Old Pete. Other suffering poor of the village impressed themselves on the mind and conscience of others.

Elder Blair and his good wife themselves set an example worthy of imitation. During the week they sought out the poor old drunkard with words of sympathy; and Mrs. Beardsley and Emma brought him food and books, and tried to win him to a better life.

They tidied up the cottage, which was rapidly falling into decay, brought over a few plants and potted some bulbs,— all this with the hope that he would at least appreciate their efforts. But it was apparently in vain. There was no human being to whom Old Pete would show anything but the surly disposition which was fast growing on him, except one: that one was not the minister, kind though he certainly was, nor Mrs. Beardsley or her gentle daughter, earnestly though they had sought to win him; it was poor little Tot Burns, the tiny sister of our ragged hero, Jet.

Tot was almost five years old,— a wayward little thing, quaint and old-fashioned, dirty and ragged. But over the poor old drunkard she possessed a power that was simply miraculous. There was nothing he would not do for the child; and as for her, "Uncle Pete," as she called him, was a hero. Of many a drink did the old man deny himself so that he might buy some gaudy toy or tempting sweetmeat for the child he loved, and the only one on earth who really loved him. Was it not Uncle Pete who always came to Tot's relief when the well-dressed and well-fed children of the neighborhood plagued and tormented her? Who mended her broken dolly, and told her stories of big Jack, the giant-killer, and held her as tenderly as her own mother — and a great deal oftener — close against his heart, till the baby eyelids would droop over the big blue eyes in the deep slumber of childhood?

But the kindly efforts of the older ones were in vain in Old Pete's behalf. However, their success was better in little Tot's family, and it was not long before Jet and Tot were members of the Sabbath-school, in good and regular standing. Through the deacon's efforts, Mr. Burns secured a good place to work, and soon the comforts of the little family began to multiply.

It was the self-imposed task of Minnie Blair to give Mrs. Burns lessons in household economy, and to teach her skill in fitting up the tiny cottage with bits of bright fancy work, which gave a cheerier look to the dreary rooms.

No one enjoyed this changed condition of things any more than Tot, and it was not long before she was explaining everything to Uncle Pete in her own peculiar way, and the old man never wearied of her childish prattle.

The hearts of children quickly receive impressions for good, and — alas, that it should be true! — for evil also. Jet and Tot soon began to show in outward looks and conduct the blessed influence which the Sabbath-school was having upon them.

One cold, snowy day, just after an unusually interesting Sabbath-school lesson had been given, Tot hurried over to see Uncle Pete, and tell him all about it. He was not entirely himself,— he was never that, lately,— but his whisky-soaked brain was certainly clear enough to comprehend that his little favorite was clambering into his arms.

"O Uncle Pete!" began Tot, utterly oblivious to the fact that he was half asleep, "you don't know who made you, does you, Uncle Pete? *I* does; an' I knows who made me an' Jet an' kitty an' everybody. The pretty lady at the Sabbus-school, she teached me an' Jet an' two, free more in my class."

The enthusiasm of the child half sobered her listener, who made an effort to be sociable.

"I 'd no idear my little gal knew so much!" he said. "Now what else do you know, little un?"

"Did I tell you who *did* make you, Uncle Pete?

God did, and Tot does like him so much, 'cause if he had n't made Uncle Pete, what *would* little Tot do?"

"Bless ye child! I dunno what Old Pete would do without ye."

"Uncle Pete, say, Uncle Pete," continued the little preacher, "*does you love God?*"

"Come, little un, let Uncle Pete tell ye a purty story," said the old man evasively. And with the golden curls pressed against the ragged sleeve, Tot listened in delighted silence, while the old man ransacked the storehouse of his memory for stories, which he told as well as he could with a thick tongue and benumbed brain. But his little listener was no critic.

"My! that was the *beautifulest* story! but you has n't told me, Uncle Pete, *does you love God?*"

CHAPTER XI.

PAUL'S SURRENDER.

IT was the Sabbath. Great flakes of feathery snow were falling, and Paul Beardsley stood by the window of his little room, and silently watched the "white bees of winter" flying swiftly downward. Now and again the wind would whisk away a whole troop of them on a mad dance up and down, hither and thither, like myriads of tiny, white-feathered arrows shot heedlessly from the bows of a whole regiment of fairy soldiers, marching up and down, here and there — anywhere, everywhere — bent on mischief.

Paul was looking at the snowflakes, and listening to the Voice. It had been speaking very loudly of late; it was pleading, O so earnestly! it was calling him to repentance.

"And the Spirit and the bride say, Come," seemed to be ringing in the air about him. "And let him that heareth say, Come," was the response. "Whosoever will, let him take the water of life freely," seemed to be sent like a message from the throne of glory to his sin-burdened soul.

Then he heard another voice,— not sweet and soft, like the first, but harsh and unmusical: "What have I to do with thee, Jesus, thou Son of the most high God?"

With a start, Paul stepped to the little table, and opened his Bible. Was it Providence? His eye rested upon a carefully marked passage in Isaiah: "Come now, and let us reason together, saith the Lord: though your sins be as scarlet, they shall be as white as snow; though they be red like crimson, they shall be as wool."

"It does n't seem as if that meant *me,*" Paul reflected. "I 've been so mean and ungrateful, and,— well, I 'm afraid if our folks knew how bad I 've been, they 'd think there was no hope for me. I tell you, Paul Beardsley," he muttered, "you 're the very *chief of sinners!* It just seems as if there was something like that in the Bible; I 'll see;" and he turned to his concordance, and found the text: "This is a faithful saying, and worthy of all acceptation, that Christ Jesus came into the world to save sinners; of whom I am chief."

"O, I don't know how anybody could say that, who never smoked cigars, and then lied about it, and never played euchre for money, nor sneaked off nights, nor made his parents unhappy and wretched,— good parents as mine are, too,— nor threatened to run away, nor,— well, it 's a mystery to me how a fellow ever could have been so worthless and wicked. I don't see how I ever can expect to be forgiven. Besides, all the town fellows would laugh at me,— I know very well Jack would. I don't suppose I could hold out,— and I hate a turncoat."

"Come now, and let us reason together," again pleaded the Voice. "When thou passest through the waters, I will be with thee; and through the rivers, they shall not overflow thee."

Paul bowed his head in his hands, and wept silently. O, *would* he yield? It was a critical moment in his life. He had been unhappy for days. Conscience had been busily at work; for one of the blessed offices of the Holy Spirit is to convince of sin. Ah, Paul! you are having a hard battle with the world, the flesh, and the devil. Who will conquer? Angels are round about you, my boy, waiting only the first word of repentance from your contrite lips. O, wait no longer! "Now is the accepted time," whispered the Voice, still loath to leave him.

"What have we to do with thee, Jesus, thou Son of God?" echoed again from the regions of darkness.

"I can never do it!" groaned the tempted lad. "I can not stand the ridicule of the boys. My temper would surely get the better of me," and he cried in anguish of spirit, *"O God, help me!"*

"It was a short prayer, not eloquent, not wordy; but it was forced from a heart which felt its bitter need. It was a cry from a perishing soul, lost on the black mountains of unbelief and sin; and such a cry never falls unheeded on the ears of the tender Shepherd. He is waiting to hear just such calls from the chief of sinners.

Paul arose, and flung himself on his knees by the side of his bed; and then ascended such a cry for pity and pardon as caused the angels to rejoice; and as they winged their way upward to repeat the glad news, such a sweet peace and sense of a Father's love and pardon came into his heart as he had never known before. God had forgiven him, and now he must ask forgiveness of his earthly father.

The snow had stopped falling, and a soft robe of fleecy white covered valley and glen, unsightly rock, and bleak and barren hillside. The old barn and shed had taken on a magic beauty, and were clothed as in bridal robes. Even their very defects, covered with this fleecy blanket, seemed only to add to their beauty.

"How like the robe of righteousness of my Redeemer!" exclaimed the happy boy.

"Father, I shall never forget how you asked my forgiveness once; now I ask yours and mother's. I don't suppose you know half my wickedness,—it would pain you very deeply if you did,—but God has forgiven me, and I know you will."

Deacon Beardsley clasped Paul's hands, and with tears of joy running down his cheeks, said softly: "'This my son was dead, and is alive again; he was lost, and is found.'"

CHAPTER XII.

A HAPPY HOME CIRCLE.

"DON'T forget about the Happy Home Circle to-night," said Emma, as she bade Minnie and Ethyl good-by after school, and hurried home so that everything might be in good order.

"Oh, no! we enjoy it too much to forget."

At seven o'clock they had all arrived, and were again seated around the big table in the pleasant sitting-room at Deacon Beardsley's.

"Well, I suppose Jack is ready to report the success of his Bible study?" questioned the deacon.

"Yes, sir. It is entirely satisfactory to me. Father laughs at me a good deal, though he himself says that the scriptures you gave me seem very plausible. Mother is pleased, but I guess it would take a good deal to make a Christian of my father."

"We'll not argue that point, Jack; only of this I am sure: 'There is none other name under heaven given among men, whereby we must be saved,'" said the deacon, impressively.

"Thank God for that," said Paul, reverently.

Jack started, and fixed an astonished look upon Paul. It was not so much his words as his manner that impressed him.

"I 've *thought* I could see a change in that boy for a few days past," he mused, "and now I 'm sure. Well, 'like father, like son.' His father 's a Christian, so of course he 'll be one; mine is n't, so I suppose that settles the case for me." Then he remembered his mother's words, when she had seen him hunting up his Bible texts: "I wish, Jack, we had all studied that blessed Book more, and lived its sacred teachings better;" and he could not help thinking of the uneasy, nervous look he had noticed on his father's face, who was in the room at the time.

These thoughts rushed through Jack's mind with the speed of lightning. All the evening, he found himself trying to remember the text the deacon had at first repeated to him, about the "name."

"What was that new game you mentioned today, Emma?" said Minnie.

"It 's one father said he used to play when he was young, so it can hardly lay claim to being a new game; but it 's nice, I think, and very instructive."

"I wonder if *we 'll* be in it," whispered Jennie to Jimmie.

"Oh, yes; but it 's pretty hard for you, I 'm afraid," said their father, who proceeded at once to explain his game. "We used to call it the Examination Game, because it was so much like a teacher's examination."

"Oh, dear! I 'm afraid I shall not pass," sighed Polly Brown.

"Well, we 'll see. You must each have slips of paper and pencil,— get them, little daughter, if you please, and pass them around. There, now, we are ready. Now, all must think of some word which begins with a certain letter of the alphabet,— we will try the letter 'A' to-night. This word must be the *answer* to some question in history, geography, Bible, grammar, or some other study. Write the word on these slips of paper; for instance, I might write 'adverb' on my slip, and Jack might write 'Abraham.' The words must all be answers to some question, and must begin with A."

In a short time all announced themselves ready to proceed. Even Jennie and Jimmie had, with tolerable skill, written each a word, which they regarded with no small degree of satisfaction.

"Now, Jimmie, suppose you and Jennie gather them all up in this little basket, and we will see what has been written, and how well we can fit question to answer."

Jennie placed the basket in her father's hand, happy to have so conspicuous a part in the big folks' game.

"Now as I read these words, you are to write the questions which these same words will answer, on these fresh slips of paper, and I can give you only one minute on each word. If, at the end of that time, your writing is not complete, you must leave it unfinished, and begin on the next. This will teach the habit of prompt thought and ready action. I see the first word which I happen to pick up in the basket is 'Augustus Cæsar.' I will help you a little with this, as it is the first. Suppose you write your question to fit it like this: 'Who was a great Roman emperor?' Then write the answer beside it, which, of course, will be the word I have just read. The next word is 'Arkansas,'" said the deacon, laying his watch on the table.

"Time's up! The next word is 'Alexander the Great,'" he soon called out; "remember you have only one minute to each word; so you must think fast. Next, 'Acropolis.'"

"Guess we can't play this game, after all, Jimmie," whispered Jennie, grasping her pencil in a very tired little hand, and wiping her forehead with the other.

"Well, never mind; we can watch the others," answered Jimmie, resignedly.

In a few minutes all the words were given out, and the answers ready.

"Now, Jimmie, you may pass the basket again, though first, I want you each to place your initials on your papers, so I can know whose they are. But as I want plenty of time to decide who has won the game by having the best answers, I shall have to ask you to be patient till another meeting. Then I propose to give the successful one a nice pocket Bible."

"Whew!" said Will Brown, with a long-drawn whistle, "I wish I'd taken more pains."

"Well," laughed Ethyl, "I'm almost glad you did n't, but I surely wish *I* had."

Jack and Will were asked to prepare something of interest for the next meeting. Just as they were about to separate, the door-bell rang.

"Why Elder Blair!" exclaimed half a dozen voices at once, "what a pity you did n't come sooner!"

"'T is too bad, but I 've been making a few calls, and just thought I 'd drop in, and see my daughter home,— but how pleasant you have it here, deacon! I guess you believe in trying to make home a happy place, and judging from the smiling faces around, I imagine you have succeeded."

"Ah, Brother Blair," said the deacon, grasping his hand warmly, "God used you as his instrument in opening my eyes; for, 'whereas I was blind, now I see.'"

CHAPTER XIII.

A TRIAL OF FAITH.

HALLO, Paul!" called Jack, the next day; "you may think it's rather odd, but I'd like to remember what that verse was,— I guess it's in the Bible,— that you father quoted last evening; may be you could tell. It was something about a name."

Paul was thankful to be able to turn at once to the text. He had of late formed a habit of carrying his little pocket Bible always with him. He handed it to Jack, who read, silently: "For there is none other name under heaven given among men, whereby we must be saved."

"There," thought Jack, "I'm sorry I said anything about it; now he'll preach to me, of course."

But he was disappointed. Paul only remarked, as he returned the sacred Book to his pocket, "*That's true,* Jack." Simple words; but they were a whole sermon in themselves. Yes, Paul *had* preached to his skeptical friend.

And the wonderful words! How they rang in the

boy's ears! Night after night, as his head pressed the pillow, these words would echo in his ears, "No other name — no other name!" It was only a verifi-

"And, pray, what are you converted to?"

cation of the promise, "My word shall not return unto me void."

One day as Paul was returning home from school, where, on account of an added lesson, he had been detained half an hour, he noticed a group of men talking and laughing on the street corner, among whom was Captain Somerville.

"Step this way, will you, young man? We were just having a little argument. I understand you 've been converted up at your house,—eh, lad?"

"I hope so, captain," replied Paul, respectfully.

"And, pray, what are you converted to?" was asked with a smile that was almost a sneer.

"To the religion of Jesus Christ, I hope," replied Paul, while a silent prayer for divine help flew with the speed of thought straight to the Father's throne.

"I suppose you young folks 'll settle down now, and not try to enjoy life any more, for fear it might be wicked, you know. Jack says you think it 's a mortal sin, now, to play a game of euchre or smoke a cigar," sneered the captain.

"Well, I 'll tell you how 't is, captain," said Paul. "I 've sold out, you know; and since then I have n't any right to do such things; but I don't want to be conscience for anybody else."

"'Sold out!'" said Bill Truman, "what do you mean by that?"

"'Ye are not your own: for ye are bought with a price: therefore glorify God in your body, and in your spirit, which are God's'—that's what I mean. Good day, gentlemen," and Paul was gone before any one could object.

"O, that boy's been trained, of course,—father's a deacon,—presume he's heard the Bible read every day of his life," said Jim Jarvis. "Anyway, that verse was right to the point."

Right to the point?—Yes; they were words which caused the sneering infidel to tremble. Ah, the sword of the Spirit, which is the word of God, is a keen weapon.

Paul felt thankful that he had been kept from disgracing the name he loved, and he resolved more earnestly than ever before to store his mind with the blessed word. The verse which had come like a swift-winged soldier to fight for him, he fully believed was an answer to his prayer for help. But he remembered that it was one he had read the evening before, little dreaming that it would serve him in such good stead so soon. O Paul! the Author of that Book has promised to bring all things to our remembrance; and they will come like well-drilled soldiers, when we need them most, if our minds are stored with their precious truths.

"Hallo! I wonder what's come over Old Pete," said Paul to himself, as he was passing the lonely house. "True as I live, he's out in the cold, mending the front gate, and he has a real large pile of wood chopped. He seems perfectly sober, too,—first time I've seen him sober in six months, I guess."

"How are you, Mr. Blake? any news from Sim?"

"Oh, no; I'll never see that boy no more. Like as not it's just as well," he added, gruffly, and turned away.

Just as Paul was moving on, thinking of the absent boy, and blaming himself for the wretched part he had once acted, he heard a soft little voice call out: "Here's Tot, Uncle Pete! Tot's goin' home wif you, if you'll tell a pretty story."

In a moment the hard old face softened, and two strong arms lifted the mite to a seat on the broad shoulder.

"Dunno what I'd do without Tot, here," said the old man, turning a face that was all lighted up, toward Paul. "She's more to me than any one ever was, an' loves me better. Say, young man, Ole Pete would do anything for this baby — *anything!* Talk about angels, h'm!" said the old man enthusiastically. "Talk about preachin'! why, this little gal preaches a sermon to me every day, don't ye, Tot?"

"Does you love God, Uncle Pete?"

The mention of "angels" and "preaching sermons" seemed to touch a responsive chord in Tot's memory at once, and bending the wise little head so that she could look full in the face of the old man, and fixing the large blue eyes lovingly upon him, she repeated her old question. "Does you love God, Uncle Pete?"

Paul thought he saw a tear in the old man's eyes; anyway, he drew the back of his hand across them quickly.

"Thank the Lord," thought Paul, as he hurried on, "the Sabbath-school is doing that child good, and I believe the child is doing Uncle Pete good."

"Well," said Deacon Beardsley that night at the supper table, when Paul had related the little incident, "'God moves in a mysterious way.'"

"I dare say she will do him more good than anything else in the world," said his wife.

"I 'm so glad," said Emma, "that God led us to work for that poor family. Jet and Tot could not be kept away from Sabbath-school now."

"Yes," assented Jimmie, "and Jet's face is always clean, and Tot 's all fixed up. Tot 's got *such* blue eyes!" continued Jimmie, admiringly.

"Say, father," questioned Jennie, to whom her father was prime authority on all religious questions, "don't you believe angels have blue eyes?"

CHAPTER XIV.

A CHAT WITH MRS. SOMERVILLE.

"COME, mother," said the deacon, "you're not feeling very well, and it 's nice sleighing this morning; let 's drive over to Elder Blair's, and consult a little about making a Christmas for the poor, hereabout,—it 's getting along toward time we were thinking of it. We can drive around through the village, and you can call and see Mrs. Somerville, while I come home."

"I don't hardly see how I can, to-day," objected Mrs. Beardsley. "I was thinking of baking, and there 's all the morning's work."

"That 's right, father; she must go; it 'll do her good. I can wash the dishes, and I guess Jennie can wipe them, before we go to school; and as for the pies and cookies, we 're a good deal better off without them than with them; that 's what Elder Blair says, and Dr. Willis, too, and I half believe they 're right. Come, now, mother, I 'll braid your hair,—she 'll be ready in a jiffy."

Emma had a decisive way lately of settling things, and Mrs. Beardsley hardly had time to object further before she found herself snugly ensconced beside her husband, well tucked in beneath the warm robes. The inspiring music of the sleigh-bells, the keen, frosty air, and more than all, the gentle thoughtfulness of her loved ones, acted like a tonic on Mrs. Beardsley, and made her feel like a new woman.

"What a help Emma 's getting to be, father!" she said; "strange are the ways of the Lord; how different life seems to me than it did one little year ago!"

"Yes, mother, we have a daughter indeed,— one for whom I feel like thanking God every day I live. Do you know, mother, she 's getting to look so much as you used to when I first knew you,— of course it only makes me love her better."

"I 'm sure she has been a great help to Paul, since — since ——"

"Since you and I began to take lessons in the Master's school of love,— is that what you mean?"

"Ah, yes, and the lessons grow sweeter with every one learned."

The consultation at Elder Blair's resulted in a decision to have a Christmas tree for the benefit of the poor children of the village, and that the presents should be paid for by little acts of self-denial by the children of more favored families.

"It will teach our children and youth a good lesson," said Mrs. Blair.

"Yes," replied Deacon Beardsley; "I am of the opinion that the little word 'self' expresses about the sum total of human wretchedness and sin. Now," continued the deacon, addressing his wife, "perhaps we would better be going, as all the arrangements seem to be pretty well made."

"Yes; I must call on Mrs. Somerville before going home," replied Mrs. Beardsley.

"I am glad you are going to see her," said Mrs. Blair; "I made her a call the other day, and she seems anxious to converse upon religious subjects,—so different from what she was when I first met her."

"She seemed the same to me, when I last called, the day of poor Mrs. Blake's funeral," said Mrs. Beardsley, as her husband helped her to a seat, and carefully covered her with the robes.

"Do you notice, my dear," smiled Mrs. Blair, as their callers drove away, "how attentive Brother Beardsley is to his wife?"

"Ah, wife, the gentle spirit of love is contagious."

Mrs. Beardsley found Mrs. Somerville very poorly indeed. She had passed a miserable night; and the dry, hollow cough, and unnaturally bright cheeks of the invalid told the sad story that consumption had marked her for its own.

"I have thought of you every day since your last visit, and I am very glad to see you to-day," said Mrs. Somerville. "I've thought so much of what you said about the great Refiner; and O Mrs. Beardsley! I am hoping that he is all this time purifying me. Do you think he is?"

"I have not the least doubt of it, my friend, and I have been wondering if it might not please him to use you as an instrument in bringing your husband and children to him."

"O, if I could only be sure that he accepts *me,* I could pray for them; but I have been a wanderer so long, I sometimes fear that the Shepherd will not receive me into his fold."

Mrs. Beardsley took the little Bible which lay on

the stand at the head of the bed, and turning to the fifty-fourth chapter of Isaiah, she read slowly, and with great earnestness: "For a small moment have I forsaken thee; but with great mercies will I gather thee. In a little wrath I hid my face from thee for a moment; but with everlasting kindness will I have mercy on thee, saith the Lord thy Redeemer."

With her thin white hands clasped, and the tears running down her cheeks, Mrs. Somerville exclaimed, earnestly, "Lord, I believe; help thou mine unbelief."

When Mrs. Beardsley left her friend that day, it was with the blessed assurance that she had been the means, in the Father's hands, of leading a weary, sin-sick wanderer to the fold of the Good Shepherd, who —

Never will cast away,
  Never will turn aside
From the prayer of the faltering lips which pray
  To the merciful Crucified.

CHAPTER XV.

ANOTHER PLEASANT EVENING.

"WELL, mother," said Emma, "it seems as if this has been the shortest month I ever spent. Minnie was asking me to-day if it was n't about time for our Happy Home Circle to meet again, and sure enough, it 's a month to-night,—queer how the time does pass! Father 's kept as still as a mouse about that prize he offered. I would n't wonder if Jack Somerville would get it. Don't you think father 's real thoughtful to select a nice Bible for a present? He does n't seem the same man he used to, anyway; does he, mother?" added Emma, who was growing to the belief that there never was just such a man as her father.

"Why, little daughter!" exclaimed the deacon, suddenly appearing upon the scene, "they say that eavesdroppers never hear any good of themselves; but I 'm quite inclined to think they are mistaken sometimes. I guess father 'll have to give you a kiss for that speech, little girl."

"Well, now, father, honestly, you *are* nicer than you used to be; come now, own up! you know it, don't you?" said Emma, returning his kiss.

"Now you know as well as I do, Emma, that to be able to *see* is a great deal 'nicer' than to be blind,—and 'whereas I was blind, now I see,'" said her father, fervently.

When seven o'clock came, the young folks were all in their places, and with an addition of two, who came with Minnie Blair. Susie Dean and her brother Fred, whose mother had died a year before, were warmly welcomed by all.

"I just thought I'd stop as I passed by, and ask them to join us, and you see I was in luck; for Mr. Dean was perfectly willing. I only wish they had been here at the last meeting, so they could have joined in competing for that prize," said Minnie.

"Well, now, I don't know," said Jack Somerville, smiling; "that would only lessen the chance of all of us, you see, and I am thinking our chairman has something pretty fine for the lucky fellow."

"I suppose you are all waiting to hear a report of the contest," said the deacon, "but I think I will defer my report until this evening's program is carried out."

"Me and Jennie, we know who 's going to get that red morocco Bible, don't we, Jen?" chuckled Jimmie, loud enough to be heard by all.

"Yes; but don't you tell Jack, Jimmie Beardsley, — don't you tell him!" said Jennie, raising her finger warningly.

"Nope," agreed Jimmie, with a determined shake of the head.

"Hush, little folks; I know who 'll not get it, nor anything else nice, I 'm afraid, if they 're not good," smiled Mrs. Beardsley.

"I suppose Jack and Will have something for us to do; we will hear from them," called the chairman.

"I believe Minnie Blair's name is down for a short essay on 'Civilization and the Bible.' Will and I thought she would be perfectly at home with such a subject," smiled Jack; and the fine essay which followed his announcement showed that their judgment was good.

"Why, Minnie Blair!" exclaimed Emma, "I 'd no idea you could write like that. Why did n't you tell me you were going to have an essay to read to-night?"

"Well, I wanted to prove to the entire satisfaction of all skeptics, that a girl can keep a secret," laughed Minnie.

"Now we will hear a song from our respected chairman and his wife," said Jack; "if they will kindly favor us."

It was Minnie's turn now to be surprised, and she turned to Polly Brown, and exclaimed in a loud whisper, "I never thought of such a thing! did you, Polly? I thought I was keeping the only secret there was!"

"I knew," smiled Polly, "because, you see, Will told me."

The song was a pathetic, old-fashioned one that Mr. and Mrs. Beardsley had sung many times when they were young. There were tears in Susie Dean's eyes when they had finished. "Poor mama used to sing that song before she left us," she said.

"Well, dear," said Mrs. Beardsley, putting an arm tenderly around her, "I hope you and we all may join her in singing a sweeter song, around the throne above, at the marriage supper of the Lamb."

"I wonder what she means by that,—these Christians are queer people," thought Jack.

"Jimmie an' me 'll have a song next time if you want us to," suggested Jennie, "won't we, Jimmie?"

"Course," assented Jimmie.

"I think our friend Paul will give us a brief description of an æolian harp," said Will.

"I thought best to make the instrument first, and then tell you just how I did it," said Paul, unwrapping a paper, and taking therefrom a long, narrow box of thin pine.

"Well, I *thought* Paul had been awfully sly lately, and now I understand it," whispered Emma.

"The æolian harp," Paul began, "was so named from Æolus, the fabled god of the winds. This box, as you see, is about six inches deep, and has a circle in the middle of the upper side, in which I have drilled small holes. Then I stretched eight strings of very fine catgut (soft, fine wire will do) over bridges at each end, like the bridge of a fiddle, which I can screw up or relax, with these screw-pins. These strings I have tuned to the key of D (low and high). Now if the wind happens to be blowing a little, we can test my instrument."

Paul then went to the window, closely followed by the twins, who were greatly excited to see Paul's "fiddle."

"I see it fits pretty well," said Paul, as he raised the sash to insert the box, which was just as long as the sash was wide. Then he raised the sash a little, to give the air admission over the strings, and the result was very soft, sweet music.

The twins were delighted. "O, is n't that splen-*difulous,* Jimmie Beardsley!"

"It *is* nice," said Jack.

"Will must make us one," said practical Polly.

"It 's lovely," added Susie Dean.

"In 1786 a man named Gattoni made an enormous instrument, called the 'Giant's Harp,' by stretching seven iron wires from the top of a tower sixty feet high to the house of a friend. In windy weather the music was very beautiful, and in a storm it could be heard for several miles."

"How poor Sim would have enjoyed all this!" sighed Mrs. Beardsley. "I feel as if the poor boy had dropped out of the world. I suppose no one has ever heard anything from him?"

"I think not." "His father does n't seem to

want to hear him mentioned. By the way, the old man does n't drink as much as he used to. It 's queer how that little Tot Burns seems to take to him; I guess the attachment is mutual."

"'And a little child shall lead them,'" smiled Minnie Blair.

"Well, now, I understand that this ends the program for to-night, so I will announce to you that, after having carefully looked over the questions and answers of last meeting, I have found that Jack Somerville has earned the prize," said the deacon, handing him a nice pocket Bible, with his name neatly printed in gold letters on the cover.

"It 's a beauty, deacon; really you are very kind. I 'd no idea when you made that offer, that I was to be the fortunate fellow. I 'm sure I shall appreciate it very much."

"It 's almost like mine," said Paul, "I am reading it by course."

"The Bible 's a pretty large book, but I think I 'll try to see what 's inside of it."

"That 's right, Jack. God bless you, my boy. I hope it will be worn out in a year," said the deacon heartily, "and if it is, I promise you I will get you another as good." Then, having voted the evening's entertainment a grand success, and with many congratulations for the happy owner of the new Bible, the little company took their departure.

CHAPTER XVI.

IN THE VALLEY OF THE SHADOW.

I MUST now ask my young readers to pass with me in imagination over the succeeding weeks of the winter, during which time nothing of note occurred in Jonesville and vicinity. We will merely stop long enough to remark that the Christmas tree for the poor children was a grand success, and that the Happy Home Circle held its regular meetings with a constantly growing interest.

It had for some time been noticed that Old Pete had been mending his ways,—he was not so liberal a patron of the saloon; in fact, he had not been seen the worse for whisky in a long time. He had given his little cottage a coat of paint, which, surrounded as it was by the bright green leaves of spring, gave it a very cozy appearance.

Little Tot was his almost constant companion, and it was wonderful what a refining and softening influence the little one had upon his rough, uncouth nature.

About this time an epidemic of scarlet fever broke out in Jonesville. Elder Blair and his wife were like ministering angels to the stricken ones.

Jimmie and Jennie had a slight attack, but thanks to good nursing, soon recovered.

Not so fortunate was poor little Tot Burns. Dr. Willis pronounced the fever of a very malignant type in her case, and gravely shook his head.

But through weary days of suffering and nights of delirium, Old Pete was a faithful and patient watcher. The weary mother worked and watched night and day, but when even she began to fail, the faithful old man stood at his self-appointed post of duty at the bedside of the little sufferer.

"It don't seem as ef God *would* let that baby die," he said one day to Mrs. Beardsley, who came to offer assistance in their hour of need. "It don't seem to me as ef he *could* let little Tot die. Do you think he will, Mis' Beardsley?" and the old man took one tiny hand, and held it in his own, caressingly.

"God's ways are best,—I can not tell. I only know that he is good and merciful," said Mrs. Beardsley.

"Do you think he would hear anybody, ef they

asked him to let her live?" he questioned with a quaver in his voice.

"Yes, yes; he would hear *you,* Mr. Blake."

"Would he hear me — *me?*" he asked, "a wuthless drunkard like Old Pete? Then I 'll ask him;" and Mrs. Beardsley saw a light in his eyes that had never shone there before.

At last the crisis drew near. Dr. Willis said that before midnight there would be a change in the little one, either for the better or the worse. About eleven o'clock that night, Old Pete was missing. It seemed a little strange to Mrs. Burns, for he had been on hand almost constantly for so long, and he knew that the next hour would bring either life or death to his little favorite.

"He tole me to let him know the minute there was a change," said Mr. Burns. "He said he was goin' home for a while. I reckon the poor man 's about worn out. He 's been a faithful old soul, he has. His heart 's sot on that child to beat all," he added feelingly.

Dr. Willis sat by the bedside, with his eyes fixed intently on the little sufferer.

"I think you would better tell the old man to step in now, if that was his wish," he said.

"I 'll step over and tell him," said Mrs. Beardsley.

There was a dim light in the window of the little cottage over the way. Mrs. Beardsley opened the door softly. The sound of an earnest voice from the next room reached her ear.

"I thought the old man would be asleep, surely. I wonder who ——" she stepped softly to the door, which was partly open, and glanced in. There was Old Pete on his knees, with trembling hands raised to heaven, and the tears raining down his face, haggard with nights of watching. Mrs. Beardsley was entirely unprepared for such a sight, and with beating heart she stood and reverently listened.

"O God, I ain't nothin' nor nobody, but that baby 's all I got, an' ef you 'll only let her live, I 'll never tech another drop of the cursed stuff long 's I live; an' I 'll try and see if I can't be a man agin. I 'll quit servin' the devil, an' I 'll be your servant always, ef only little Tot may live. O, I b'lieve she will! an' Old Pete thanks ye with all his heart."

It seemed to the astonished visitor at the door that an angel had entered the little room. The face of the earnest suppliant was almost transfigured as he rose from his knees.

"Is that you, Mis' Beardsley? I 'm ready to go 'long with ye now. I 'd no ideer God would be so willin' to hear a wuthless old man like me; but he did, Mis' Beardsley, he did, an' Old Pete never 'll be ongrateful enough to forgit it."

They opened the door of the darkened room, softly. The anxious watchers were too intent upon noting the gray shadows as they flitted across the little pinched face, to notice the light which shone in the old man's eyes.

"Thank God, Mis' Burns, the little gal 's goin' to stay with us. Yes, Doc, Old Pete 's asked Him, an' he 's goin' to let her."

Mrs. Burns looked up quickly, fearful that so much worry and anxiety had told on the old man's brain.

Just then the little one opened her eyes, and sighed softly.

"I guess you are right," said Dr. Willis, turning to the old man, and laying his hand gently on the little forehead. "See! she has fallen into a quiet sleep, now, and the most she will need hereafter is good nursing."

"Never fear for that, Doc, while Old Pete lives," was the earnest reply, as he took up his old station in a chair at the bedside of his little favorite.

"Out of the mouth of babes and sucklings thou hast perfected praise," said Mrs. Beardsley, as she walked slowly homeward in the gray of the morning.

And so little Tot lived, and before many days was growing strong. But that a great change had come over Uncle Pete was very apparent, even to the most skeptical. Elder Blair heard the news with glad thanksgiving. "'This my son, was dead, and is alive again; he was lost, and is found.' There is surely joy among the angels of heaven."

"What! Old Pete converted!" exclaimed Captain Somerville. "Ridiculous! he 'll be as full of whisky as ever in less than a month."

But month after month rolled by, until a year had passed; and still the keeping power of God proved to be enough even for such as he. Uncle Pete was a model of propriety, and he might be seen almost any evening with little Tot on his lap, telling her Bible stories about the "great God, who saved yer life, little Tot."

There was no one more regular in his attendance at divine service than the happy old man. Elder Blair secured the position of sexton for him; and every one thought it was gratitude for this which prompted the testimony he always bore: —

"'I 'd rather be a doorkeeper in the house of my God, than to dwell in the tents of wickedness.'"

It was a balmy evening toward the last of June. The air was soft and sweet with the perfume of roses, and the great red sun was just sinking into a bed of crimson and purple. Uncle Pete sat in the door of his cottage. You would hardly know him now. His clothes were neat and clean, and the kindly face was lit up with the peace of God. His Bible was upon his knee, open at the story of the prodigal son. Little Tot was playing near him. He had been reading the story aloud: "But when he was yet a great way off his father saw him, and had compassion, and ran, and fell on his neck, and kissed him."

"I wonder where *my* poor boy is. I believe I 'll go and meet *him*." To say and resolve was to do, with Uncle Pete, as people called him nowadays ; and calling the child to him, the old man told her all about it,— it was a habit of his,— and Tot's wise little head began to lay plans at once.

"Yes, Uncle Pete, I can't hardly spare you, but then I s'pose God wants you to go an' find Sim."

"So he does, Tot, an' I tole him ef he 'd let ye live, I 'd always do as he wanted me to."

The next morning, Elder Blair was surprised to receive a call from the old man, before breakfast.

"I 'll tell ye, parson, the Lord wants me to go an' hunt up that boy o' mine; so I 'm thinkin' ye 'd better speak for another sexton."

"God bless you, Uncle Pete ! Have you heard from the poor boy?"

"No, parson, no ; I only wisht I had. But I shall find him,— yes, I shall find him. I never could die easy till I see my poor boy. I never sot much store by him, but I 'll find him, an' he 'll forgive me," and the old man smiled hopefully through his tears.

"Where do you mean to go first?" said Mrs. Blair.

"Go ? take the midnight train for Chicago, like

my poor boy done. He 's out West somewheres, an' I 'll find him. Good-by, parson."

"Good-by; may the Lord lead you, uncle," said Elder Blair, while his wife turned to brush away a tear.

"O, he will, parson, he will. Seems like I could n't leave Tot; but I 'll be back an' bring my boy with me."

"'According to your faith be it unto you,'" said Mrs. Blair, reverently, and the old man was gone.

It was a seven days' wonder in Jonesville when everybody learned that Uncle Pete was really gone, and, as Madam Grundy expressed it, "after that scapegallus of a boy. Silly old man! he must be getting crazy." But Deacon Beardsley only shook his head, and said, "Whereas he was blind, now he sees. Praise the Lord."

* * * * *

The summer passed rapidly by, and with the first touch of flame which the coming of September brought to the leaves of the sumac and maple, Mrs. Somerville began to fail rapidly. One afternoon a messenger came to Mrs. Beardsley in great haste, saying that Mrs. Somerville was very much worse, and wanted to see her.

Dr. Willis stood by the bedside when Mrs. Beardsley entered. There was an anxious look on his face.

"The captain would send for you, doctor, but it 's of no use this time. My days are numbered," the invalid was saying, feebly. "O Mrs. Beardsley! I am so glad you have come ! Yes, dear friend, my days are numbered, and I am ready to go."

Ethyl stood at the foot of the bed weeping, while Jack sat disconsolate by the bedside. Captain Somerville sat with the thin, white hand in his own, while an expression of utter hopelessness rested upon his face; for he saw that his beloved wife was surely passing away from him, and he had not the sweet hope which was an anchor to her soul in this hour of bitter trial. He only saw her going into the dark beyond, where to him was nothing but blackness and the shadow of death.

A look of sweetest resignation rested upon the white face of the dying woman. "My dear friend," she said, fixing her large, lustrous eyes, bright with the fire of faith and hope, upon Mrs. Beardsley, "I wish you would take the good Book, and read to me. I want you to read at the place where the Book is opened. It is the last I was able to read. You led me to my Saviour, and it will seem sweet to hear your voice and his speaking to me."

"'I am the resurrection, and the life: he that believeth in me, though he were dead, yet shall he live.'" Mrs. Beardsley's voice faltered.

"'The resurrection and the life,'" softly murmured the fast stiffening lips.

"Thank God!" said Dr. Willis, reverently.

"Jack, my poor boy, it's not much mother ever was able to do for you; but don't forget that I prayed for you with my last breath. And O, I entreat you, remember that 'there is none other name under heaven given among men, whereby we must be saved.'"

They were the very words that were always ringing in his ears. How strange that his dying mother should make use of them!

"Ethyl, my dear girl, I feel sure that my prayers will be heard for you. Give your heart to the Saviour early in life. My only regret is that I did not do so sooner.

"Behold! He Prayeth."

"My husband," and the eye of the dying woman kindled with prophetic fire, "my beloved one, something tells me that I need not fear for you. Last night, in my dreams, I was praying for you, and I heard a voice sweeter than music say: 'Fear not; he is a chosen vessel unto me; for, behold, he prayeth.'"

Captain Somerville fell on his knees at the side of the bed.

"O God, have mercy!"

"'Behold, he prayeth;'" murmured the dying woman; and with a smile of joy and triumph, she whispered, "'I am the resurrection and the life.'"

"Amen," responded Dr. Willis. But the feet had already entered the river, and the ear was deaf to the sounds of earth, till the voice of the archangel and the trump of God shall awaken the sleeper to life and immortality.

"O my boy! My poor Sim!"

CHAPTER XVII.

AFTER MANY DAYS.

NOW, boys and girls, I will ask you to go with me to a little cabin on the broad prairies of the West. It is not such a comfortable home as that in which most of my readers live. There are no carpets upon the floor, and no pleasant pictures adorn the walls. The light is admitted by a single window in one side; and the floor, worn hard and firm by the feet, is not covered with nicely matched boards. The sun is hanging low in the west, and great banks of dark clouds entirely obscure it at times, and now and then a sudden gust of wind speaks of a coming storm. It is late in the autumn, and the grass of the prairie is parched and dry. Look! a traveler is coming in the distance. Something in his appearance seems strangely familiar. We notice, as he draws nearer, that he is weary and travel-worn, and there is a look of intensest anxiety upon his face. He is nearer still now, and we can see his face plainly. What! is this Uncle Pete? The effect of years of dissipation and hard drinking is still plainly visible, but the kindly gray eyes shine with the peace of heaven; and the trembling hand, which shakes as with palsy as he knocks on the door, tells of the anxiety of the old man. Time after time he repeats the knocking, and still there is no response.

"I kinder guess this is the place," he says to himself, looking up at the cloudy heavens, and noticing the growing darkness. "It 's goin' to be a pretty sharp shower, 'pears to me. I might as well stop under this back shed a while; maybe somebody 'll come 'long bimeby. O, if I kin only find my poor boy!" and the old man steps around the hut, and looks long and earnestly over the prairie in every direction. But his unaccustomed eye does not see the figure of a horseman outlined against the fast darkening sky.

"I jest kinder believe that boy ain't fur off. The man I met described my Sim to a dot, an' he said he was a-stoppin' here," sighs Uncle Pete, as he sits down on a rough bench under the shed. The rain begins to fall in great sheets, as he crouches under the rude shelter. After a time he drops upon his knees, and pours out his soul in earnest prayer. He arises filled with new faith and courage. It seemed afterward as if an angel had come to strengthen him for the hour of darkness and bitterness before him.

Suddenly a horse's impatient neigh breaks the stillness. It is the work of a moment for Uncle Pete to rush out in the rain, while a premonition of impending trouble makes him sick at heart. A horse stands beside the rude shed, which had evidently served as a stable. The bridle is dangling loosely from the neck of the animal, which Uncle Pete can see at once has been ridden hard for some distance. It does not take the old man long to conclude that the rider must surely have been thrown from the saddle and perhaps killed, or that at least some accident has befallen him. With a quick prayer for help, he mounts the tired animal, and sets off down the road in the direction from which he judges the horse has come.

The rain has stopped falling, and the moon occasionally shows her face from behind masses of broken and jagged clouds. Suddenly a gleam of moonlight reveals a dark object lying close beside the road. Yes, it is the rider,— the old man is sure of that. Is he dead? Uncle Pete's heart beats hard, and his hand trembles, as he leaps to the ground, and, bending over the prostrate figure, turns the face upward. Just now the moon comes out, and shines with a pale light upon it. The old man sinks upon his knees, and gasps, "O my boy! my poor Sim!" Ah! there 's a large bottle by his side,— it has been broken by the fall, but it tells a sad and only too familiar story to the heart-broken old man who stoops over him.

It is a task to lift the almost unconscious figure, and place it upon the horse, but it is done; and with a sorrowful heart, Uncle Pete starts for the little cabin. Here he sits through the long night and till noon of the next day, keeping sorrowful watch over his son until he awakes from his drunken slumber.

Well does the old man know that it is the drink from the black bottle, which so unsteadied his poor boy's brain that he could not keep his seat upon the back of his faithful horse. Besides, the fall to the ground had stunned him, so he would certainly have been unable to reach the cabin that night.

At last the dull eyes open, and stare vacantly around.

"O Sim! Sim, my poor boy! don't you know your father? I'm goin' to save ye, Sim; I've come for ye. Granny's dead,—did ye know it, boy? died callin' arter poor Sim. We're all 'lone now, boy, you 'n' me. You'll go 'long back with yer old father, won't ye Sim? God's forgive me, an' I know my boy will."

A look of hardness and bitterness steals over the face of the miserable boy; the shock sobers him.

"So you've got good, eh? How long'll it last—till you can get another drink? You're too late to help me. Blood tells,—yes, blood tells; 'like father, like son'—'chip o' the old block.' Where's my bottle? I must have the drink—I tell you *I must, I will!*" he exclaims fiercely.

It is a long time before the heart-broken old man can persuade him to be quiet; but when at last he succeeds, there follows a long, long talk.

Sim and a chum of his had been staying at this place, which had been deserted by the ranchmen, who had been forced by starvation to abandon it, and Sim had intended to join his companions in the next town that very day.

Tearfully the old man tells him of the weary months of patient search for his boy, how he would never give him up, and how at last he had struck a clue which led to the sad reunion. He tells him the particulars of his grandmother's death. of her faith that he would come back sometime, of little Tot, and of his own conversion; but his listener is morose, and finally silent.

It is late at night before Uncle Pete can close his eyes in slumber. Would he be able to persuade the poor, misguided boy, after all, to return home with him? and even if he did, what would be the result? Bitter anguish of spirit fills his heart, and almost overwhelms him. He feels that his punishment is greater that he can bear. He listens to the heavy breathing of his son, on his hard bunk, hardly yet recovered from the effects of his drunken spree; and memory takes him back to that desolate night when he himself was in the same condition, and when his poor boy stole from the home that should have been a shelter to him, to become a wretched wanderer on the earth. Then from his breaking heart there arises a prayer for grace and pity and strength in this hour of bitter need.

At last, sleep comes to the weary man. The morning sun streams into the little window before he awakes. His first thought is of Sim. He glances over to his bunk of straw. *It is empty!* The old man's heart sinks and throbs with a sickening dread. Then he reasons more calmly. Of course it can not be that the boy has gone. It must be that he is just outside, attending to the horse. Quickly the old man rises. His eye catches sight of a scrap of paper pinned to the door. His hand trembles so that he can hardly hold the paper, and there is such a mist before his eyes that it is some time before he can read the cruel message scrawled upon it: —

"Don't trouble to come any farther. I'm gone

for keeps, this time. If you 'd begun a little earlier, — but you did n't. Your preaching and praying are a little too late now. I love the drink,— the drink of hell,— and I must have it. Do you know of any one that I take my taste after? Well, then, don't trouble to curse me; you 've done that all your life, and it 's all you ever have given me except this horrible thirst. Of course I 'll wind up in the ditch, or worse; but who cares? If you have ever missed mother's picture, don't hunt for it. I intend to keep that much,— it 's mine. She 's the only one on this green earth who ever loved me; you see I don't believe your pretensions — not much. If there is a God, he has forsaken me. I will not go home with you. Tell the old neighbors you came a little bit too late. I hope every one who ever knew me will forget

"SIM BLAKE."

It took the old man a good half-hour to read the paper, and when he had finished, he looked years older. It seemed as if he could not possibly be the same Uncle Pete who had entered the cabin door so hopefully, though so anxiously, only the day before.

It was a poor wreck of a man, indeed, that at last reached Jonesville, and entered the cozy little home which he had left months before. But God did not forsake him, and he was wonderfully sustained by the almighty arm of him who pitieth them that fear him, as a father pitieth his children. Nor did God forsake the poor wanderer. It is his Spirit that keeps fresh in the boy's mind that last long talk with his father, and will not let it be forgotten. It is that same tender and longsuffering Spirit that brings up before him memories which he fain would banish, and that finally, after years of dissipation and wretchedness, conquers the poor prodigal, and wins a glorious victory.

* * * * *

More than ten years have passed away since my young readers became acquainted with some of the people of Jonesville,— years that have brought with them many changes.

"What became of Sim Blake, finally? Did he ever come back home?" and "What about Captain Somerville, and Jack, and Ethyl;— yes, and the Beardsley family — all of them?" I can almost hear from hundreds of anxious young readers, who have followed them patiently through their many experiences.

Let us take a peep into the old home of Deacon Beardsley, which has grown so familiar to us, and see if we can learn something more about our old friends.

Ten years have brought many changes. Who is this tall young woman, with mild manners and sweet voice? If you look closely, I dare say you will agree with me that it is our little friend Jennie. It is Christmas day, and the deacon has just come in from the barn, and taken a seat by the cheerful fire. His hair and beard are white as the flakes of snow which are slowly falling, and the stoop in the broad shoulders is much more noticeable than when we first saw him. But the rugged face is beautiful, despite its threescore and five years; the peace of God has long rested there.

The table is set carefully and daintily as on that memorable day when Paul was seventeen. But the loving mother hands which prepared the food *that* day are folded and at rest. The arm-chair where she sat so many years is empty now, and the familiar rooms which were made sacred by her gentle presence seem to miss it still.

"Well, Jennie, girl, is everything all ready? I

guess I 'll just call Jimmie. They 'll surely be here soon, now," says the deacon, briskly. Hark! there is a loud ring at the front door. Jennie flies to open it, followed by a manly, red-cheeked youth, who has just come in at his father's call, and who so closely resembles Jennie that we are sure at once that Jimmie is alive and well. The door is opened by eager hands, and in another moment a tall, bearded man has our Jennie in his arms,—wait! there is some one just behind him. The same sweet blue eyes that we remember so well, we are sure must belong to our dear Emma. Shall we attempt to describe this meeting? Does it not seem to the reader, even as it does to the writer, far too sacred a task? Suffice it then to say that it is a joyous one, saddened only by the thought of the dear one whose empty chair is a constant reminder of her.

"How lovely you have grown, father! your hair and beard are so beautifully white!"

"O Emma! you are at your old tricks, I see. You are the same little girl that used to say, 'Father 's a darling.'"

"I declare, Paul," said Emma, "it does n't seem possible that our twins could have grown so tall and large. Why, let 's see; it 's nearly six years since we left home for the mission."

"Yes, it 's six years since mother died, and you left for India soon after," said the deacon, wiping away the tear, which fell and glistened on the white beard. "Ah, that was a lonely time, but God's grace was sufficient."

"Come, this is no time for sadness," said Paul, with a tremble in his voice. "We have every reason to thank God for his great goodness to us."

"O, yes! and Jennie and Jimmie are such treasures! I don't know what I 'd do without them," said the deacon.

"We have invited Elder Somerville and his wife to take dinner with us," said Jennie. "I think it 's time they were coming now," she added, looking out of the window.

"How thoughtful of Jennie! We shall be so glad to see them."

"Jack fills the same old pulpit that Brother Blair used to preach from when you were children; and he fills it acceptably, too," said the deacon. "There have been a number of accessions to the church since he became its pastor. He 's young yet; but he gives promise of being one of our best laborers. I am sure the Lord is using him to his glory."

"There they come now!" cried Jennie, rushing to the door. Again I shall leave the meeting of these old friends to the individual imagination of the reader. But as they seat themselves about the table to partake of the good things which have been prepared by the skilfull hands of our Jennie, we will listen to the conversation. We listen reverently to the voice of the white-haired old man, trembling with emotion, as he asks the blessing of Heaven upon the food and upon his flock. As upon that occasion so well remembered by them all,— the turning-point of Paul's life,— he mentions them each by name, and as on this former occasion, Paul turns his head to hide the gathering tears; for he knows that his father's thoughts are of the one vacant chair.

"It seems as if I can never call you by any other names than Jack and Minnie," said Emma, turning to their honored and beloved guests.

"You need not do so, my girlhood's best-loved friend," smiled Mrs. Somerville.

"Paul and I are anxious to hear the particulars

of the captain's death," said Emma. "We have had only very meager news of him."

"Of course you know he died in London, last June, at a mission he had founded five years ago. O, my mother's prophecy was so well proved to be

He knows that his father's thoughts are of the one vacant chair.

true that I consider it a direct revelation from God; for, indeed, he was a 'chosen vessel.' His death was caused directly from a severe attack of pneumonia, brought on by overwork and exposure; for he never knew what it was to rest, after his conversion. 'I must redeem the time,' was his motto. His last words," added the young parson, through his tears, "were those blessed ones of Paul, 'I have fought a good fight, I have finished my course, I have kept the faith.'"

"Thank God!" murmured the deacon.

"I was just thinking," said Jack, "that the little morocco Bible you gave me so long ago was one of the instruments God used in my conversion."

"Thank God," again responded the deacon. "'Whereas I was blind, now I see.'"

"I hope Ethyl will come over to-morrow; I am anxious to see her," said Emma.

"I think she intends to. She is very much interested in her Sabbath-school work. You remember little Tot Burns; she is one of Ethyl's most intelligent scholars. But she will never cease to mourn for Uncle Pete."

"Yes," said Paul, "Jennie wrote us that he died with Tot's hand in his, praying for Sim, and murmuring the same old testimony: 'I had rather be a doorkeeper in the house of my God, than to dwell in the tents of wickedness.'"

"I suppose you have heard of Sim's grand success in the lecture field," said Jack; "the temperance people have engaged him for the winter. He will never cease mourning for his father, who died you know, some time before Sim's conversion and return home. Poor old man! he always believed his prayers would prevail for Sim."

"What good news!" said Paul. "The Lord's ways are wonderful and past finding out. I hardly believed the old man would find him that time when he started out; but the Lord led him, and in Sim's conversion we have a wonderful example of the power of a father's love."

"Yes," said the deacon, "Sim could never forget the self-sacrificing love that prompted that journey."

"What about Polly Brown, and Will, and Susie, and Fred Dean?"

"Polly and Susie are teachers in the village school, Will is the principal, while Fred is on the old farm. None are converted, but we are praying for them," said the young pastor, earnestly. "With God all things are possible."

And now the meal is ended, Paul excuses himself, and again, as of old, makes his way to his dear old room. Jennie has kept it in much the same condition as when he last saw it. Even the rose-colored curtains are the same tint as of old. He stands by the window, and, as on the Sabbath afternoon of his conversion, so many years ago, again watches the feathery flakes of snow fall gently earthward. He thinks of the past, with its many vicissitudes, and of the future, glorious with its possibilities of a grand work for the Master; and, best of all, of the "by and by," when the work shall all be ended, and of the blissful meeting of loved ones over there. The open Bible is lying upon the stand; Paul takes it and reads aloud: "In my Father's house are many mansions."

FINIS.